AF261178

First published in 2021 by Annalese Press
134 Towngate
Netherthong
Holmfirth
West Yorkshire HD9 3XZ
England

Cover and interior artwork by Peter Wadsworth
Cover painting: *The Mirror of Venus* by Sir Edward Coley Burne-Jones,
The Gulbenkian Foundation, Lisbon, Portugal.
Other artwork:
La Dame à la licorne, Musée de Cluny in Paris
Study of a Female Figure with Rosary and *The Crystal Ball*,
John William Waterhouse
Portrait of a Girl, Egypt, mid 4th Century A.D., Prague
Saint Michael, Pellegrino di Giovanni, Museum of Fine Arts, Boston
Study of Head, Fergus Firth
Ceramic Sculptures, Toni Thomas

British Library Cataloguing-in-Publication Data
A catalogue record for this book is available on request from the
British Library.

ISBN 978-1-9163620-3-1

In the Kingdom
of
Longing

In the Kingdom of Longing
nothing seems to last forever
hills turn rust to ruin
forests arise then vanish
fortune wears a paper tent

I kiss you as you fly
want to become more than nameless
the girl in a thin dress

as if April arrives starstruck
denies nothing of her sweetness
comes ribboned
scarlet and pink
faithful.

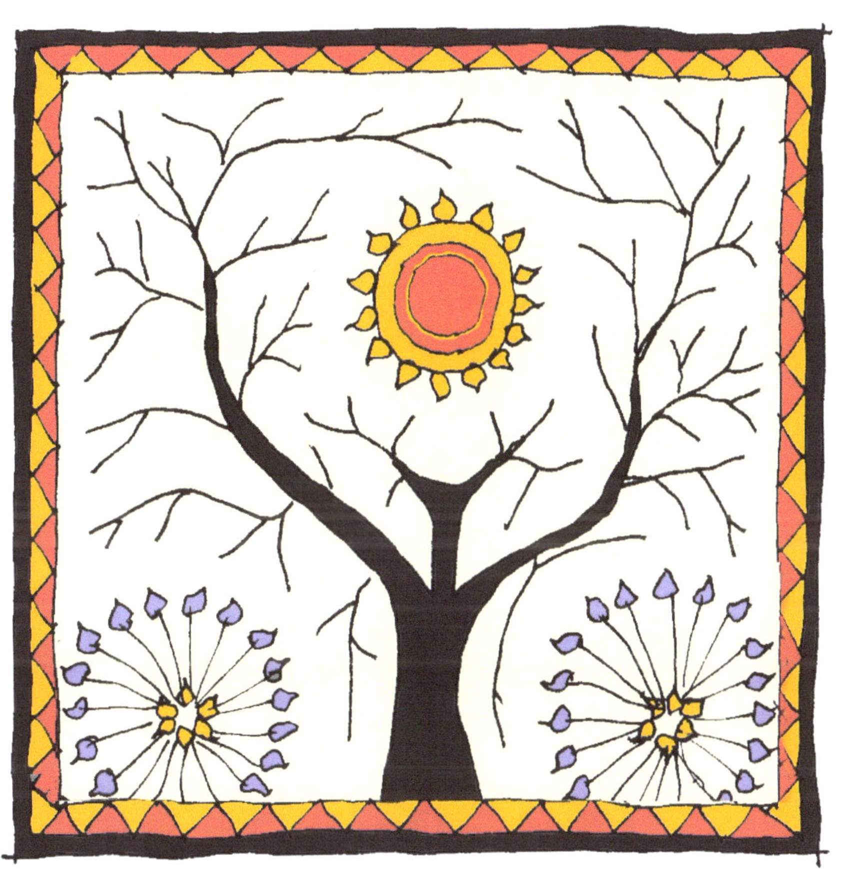

In
the
Beginning

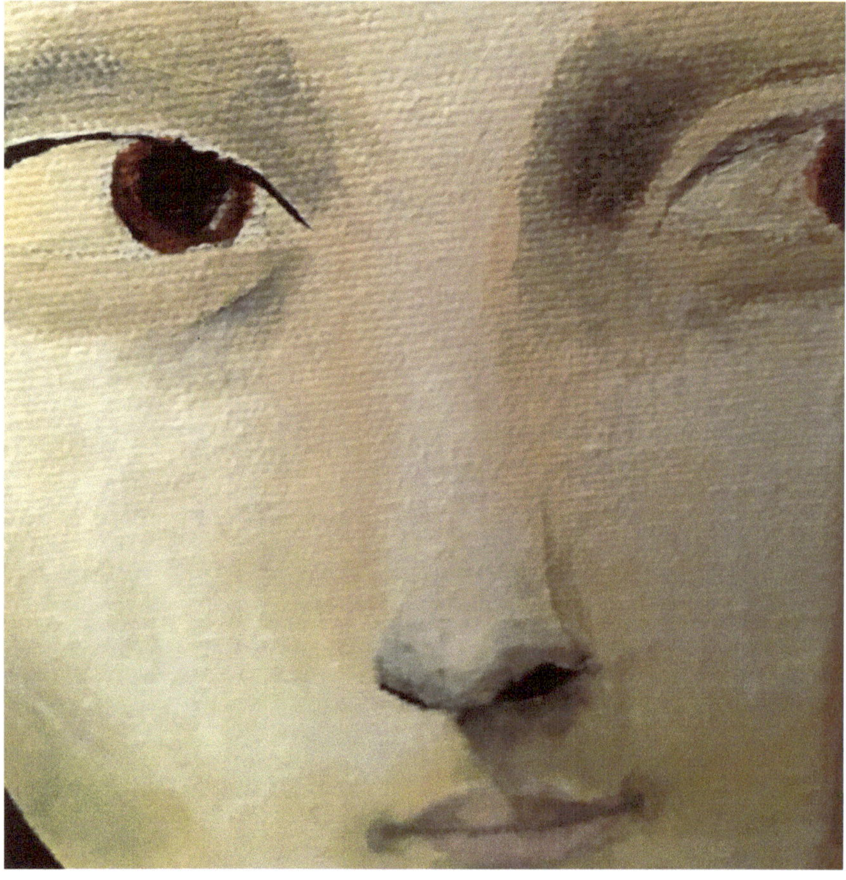

In the beginning
there was the word
and the word rang through
the sun glazed field
fingered the wind
the trees
slumbered the fox
vouchsafed the meadow.

Nothing was pronounced
unholy.

You lodge between
the table and sill
the toast and the plate
flavour my tea.
I am yours by temperament
and attrition
feather and flight.

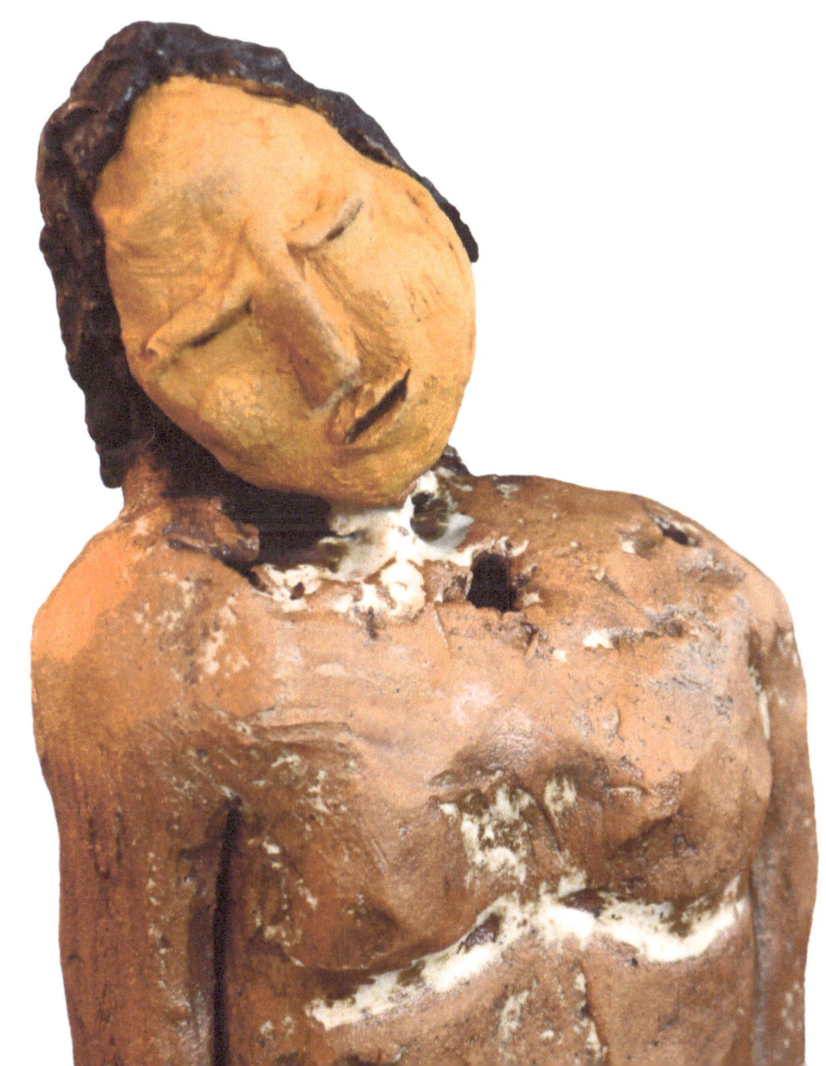

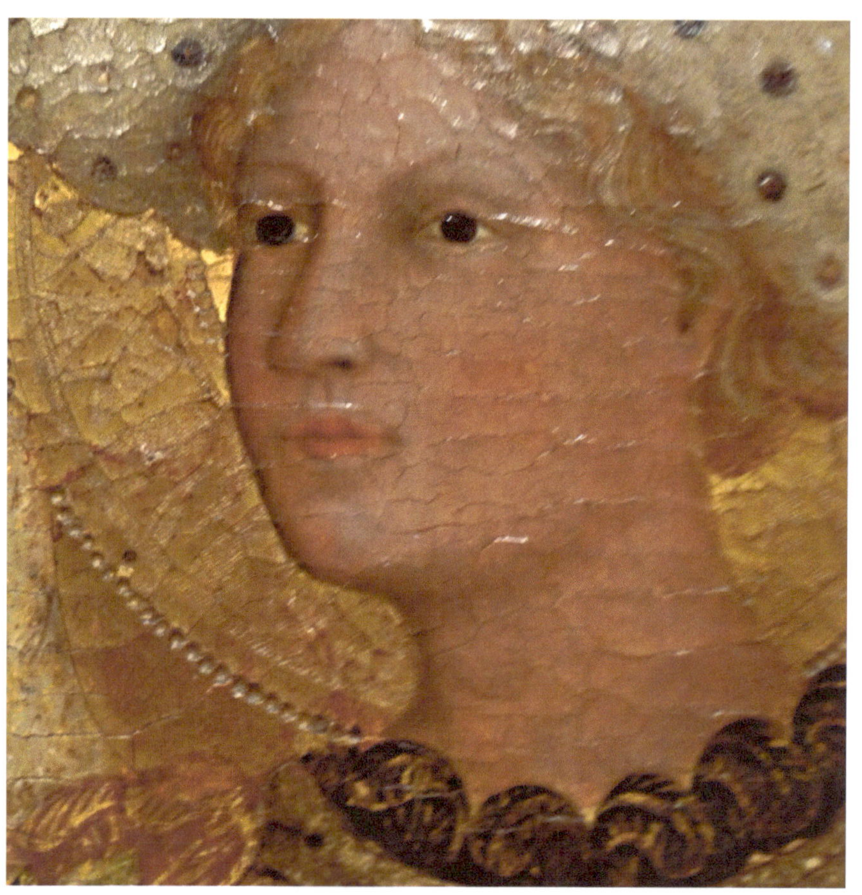

What colour is holiness
where does it come from
how can I tempt it to stay?

Finches chatter
nibble our seed.
The sky unbuckles morning.
Steam rises from the field.
My heart carries your salt
carries your salt.

The shy songstress
your voice moistens the rain
plants stars across my window.

How can I be vagrant
arrive not
with the gift of peaches?

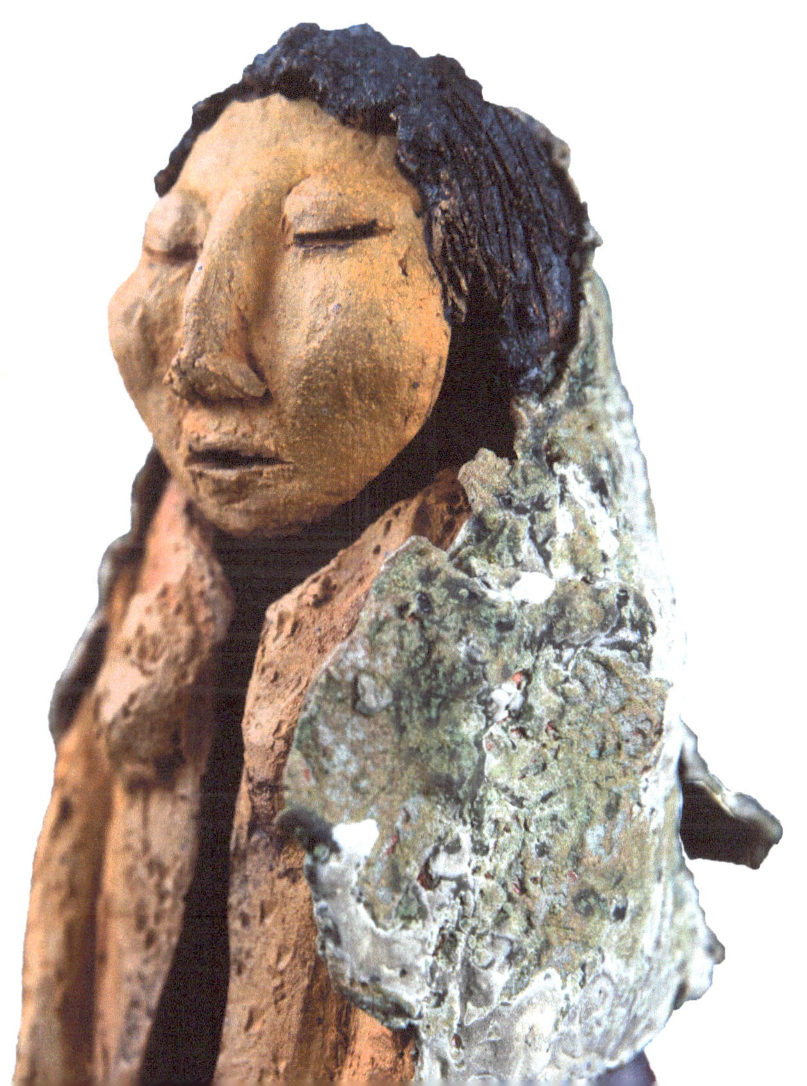

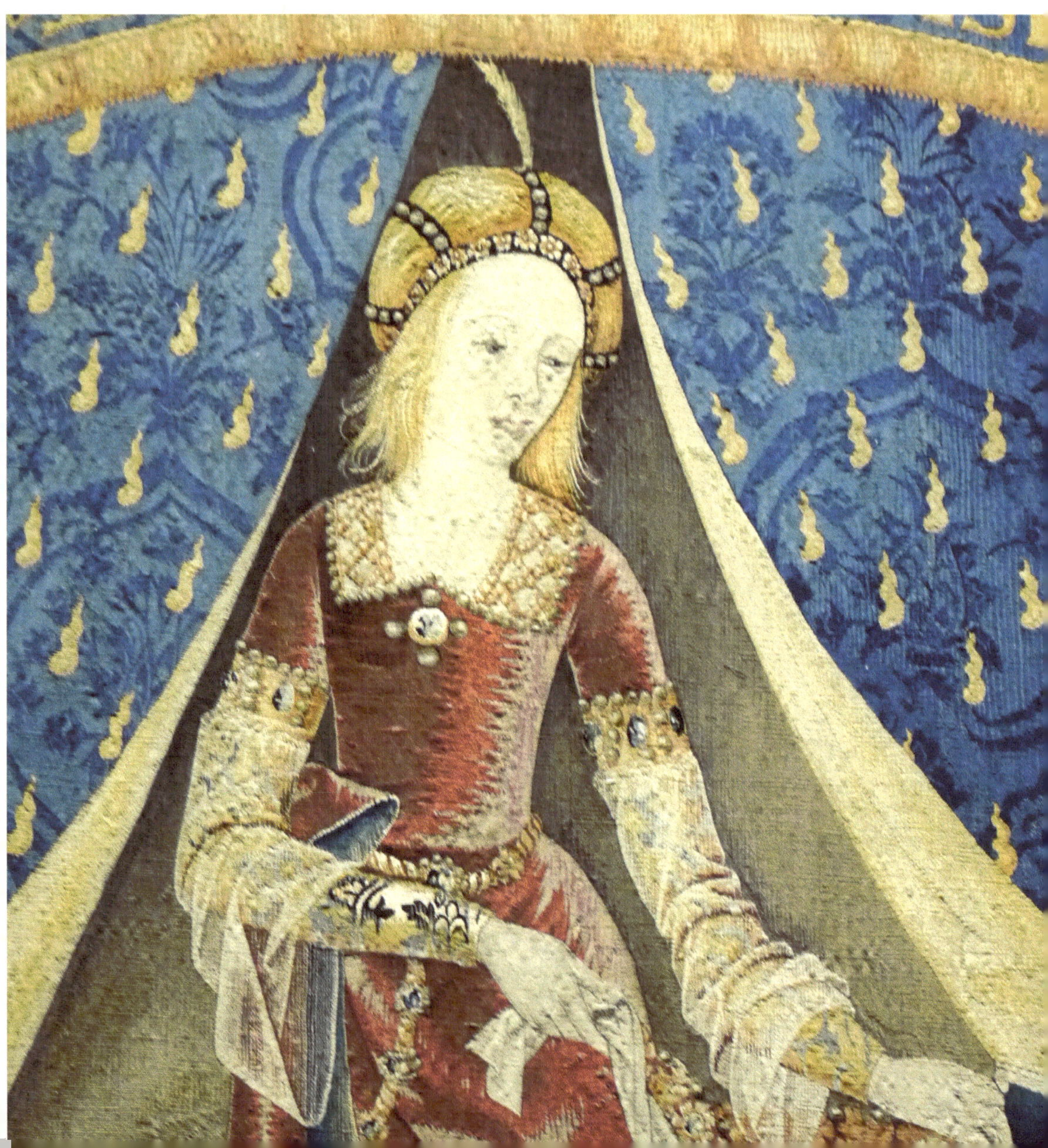

Inside the amber grain
the snow's lacework
the ribboned river
I taste the color
of your body.

You are the spoon and cake
first ray of sun
nightfall and nectar.
Hungry as the bee
I circle you.

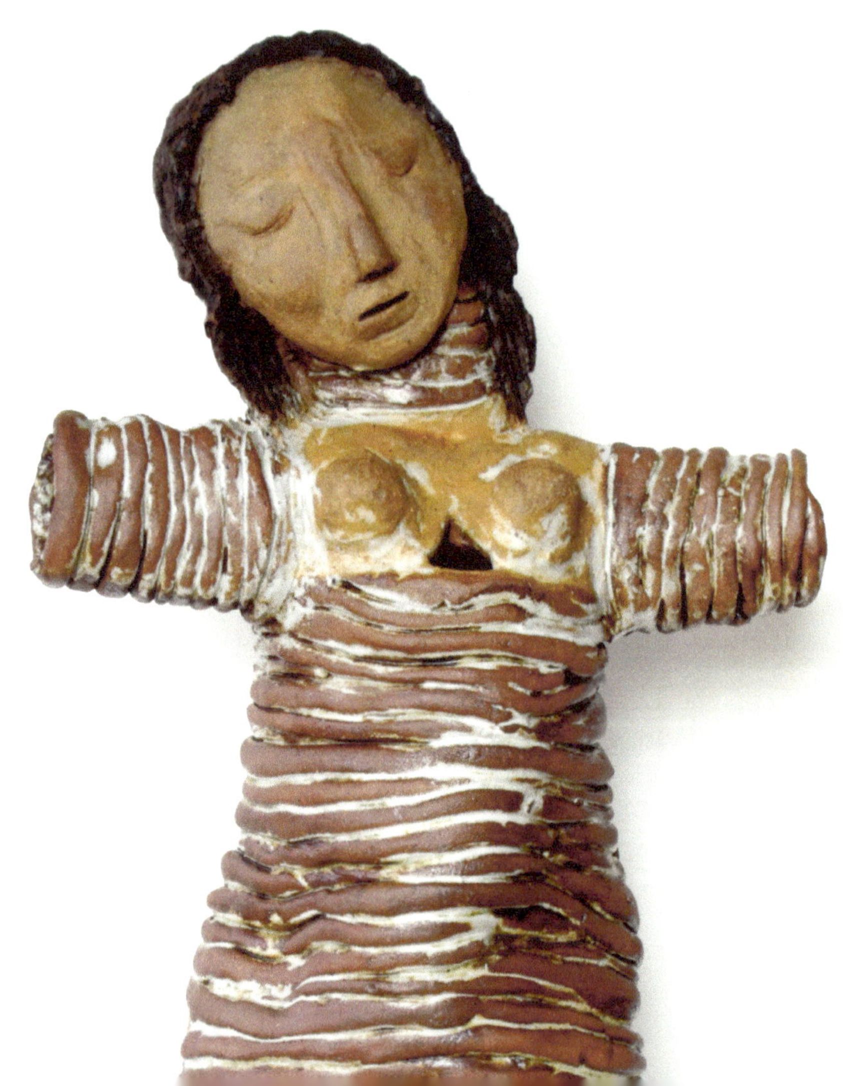

Beyond choice
my body sets table
offers up pomegranates
eats from your plate.

I nap in your crevices
want to learn the language
of goose, possum, quail
stay faithful.
Even when I sleep
your hands rehearse me.

Amid the hundred thousand things
you weave a nest
as if we are precious
the snowy plover
star inked lake
moon's splash pool.

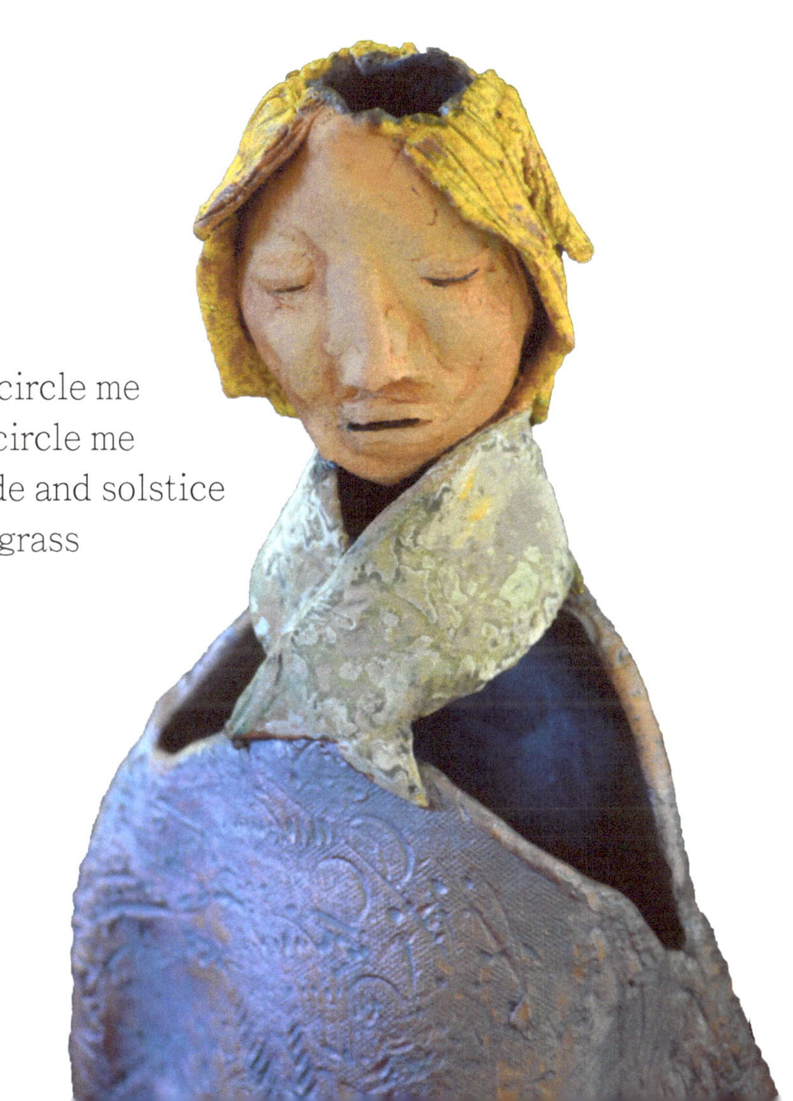

You encircle me
you encircle me
serenade and solstice
unruly grass
wind.

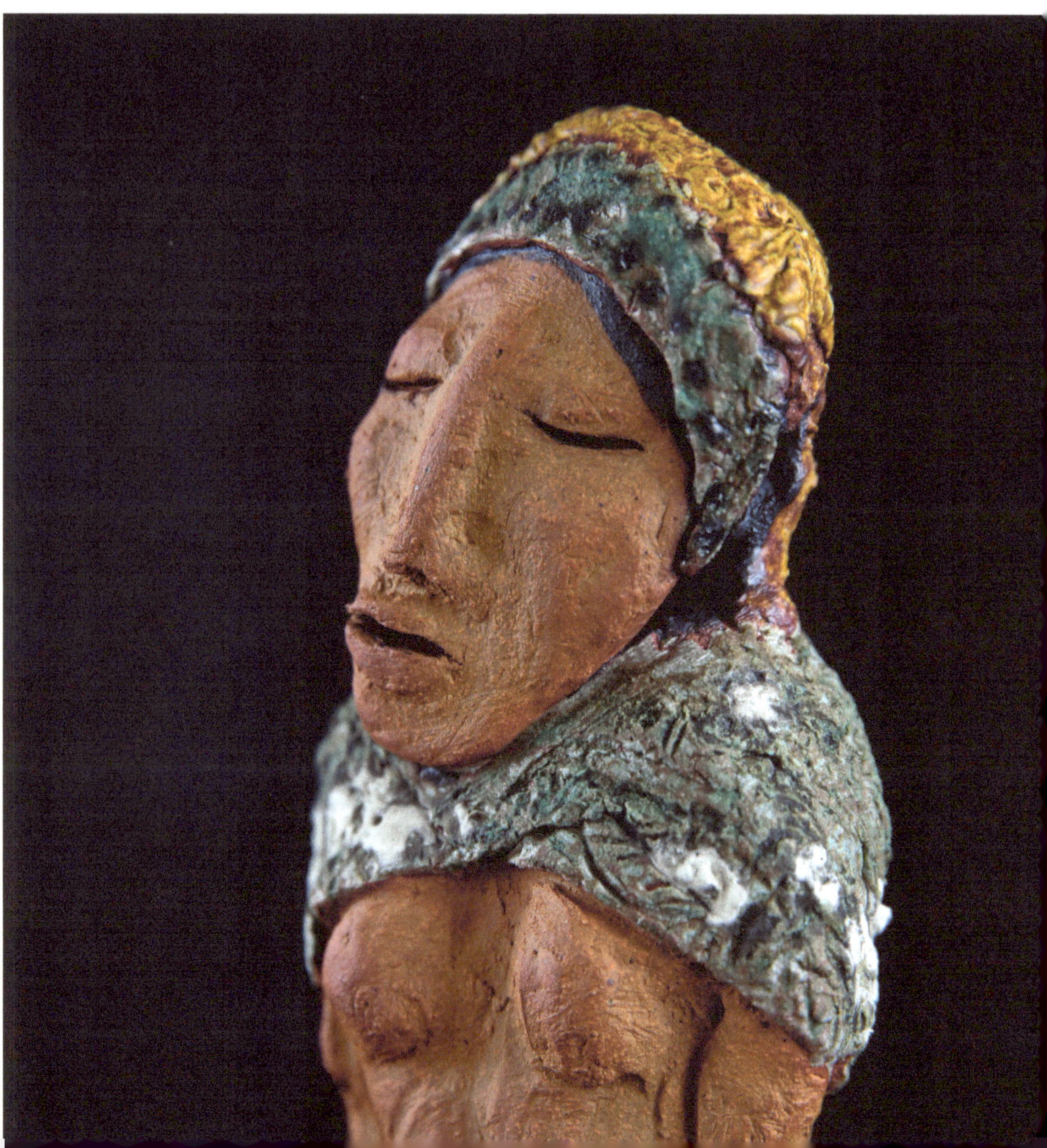

Tell me -
does every flower
unfold as a kiss?

This day is the crazed worship
of poppy, fig leaf
turnip and leek.
This day is rain and metal
so many paths to the well.

Outside my window
the fig leaves unspool
honeysuckle climbs
the girl in the thin dress
eats snow
is crowned by birds.

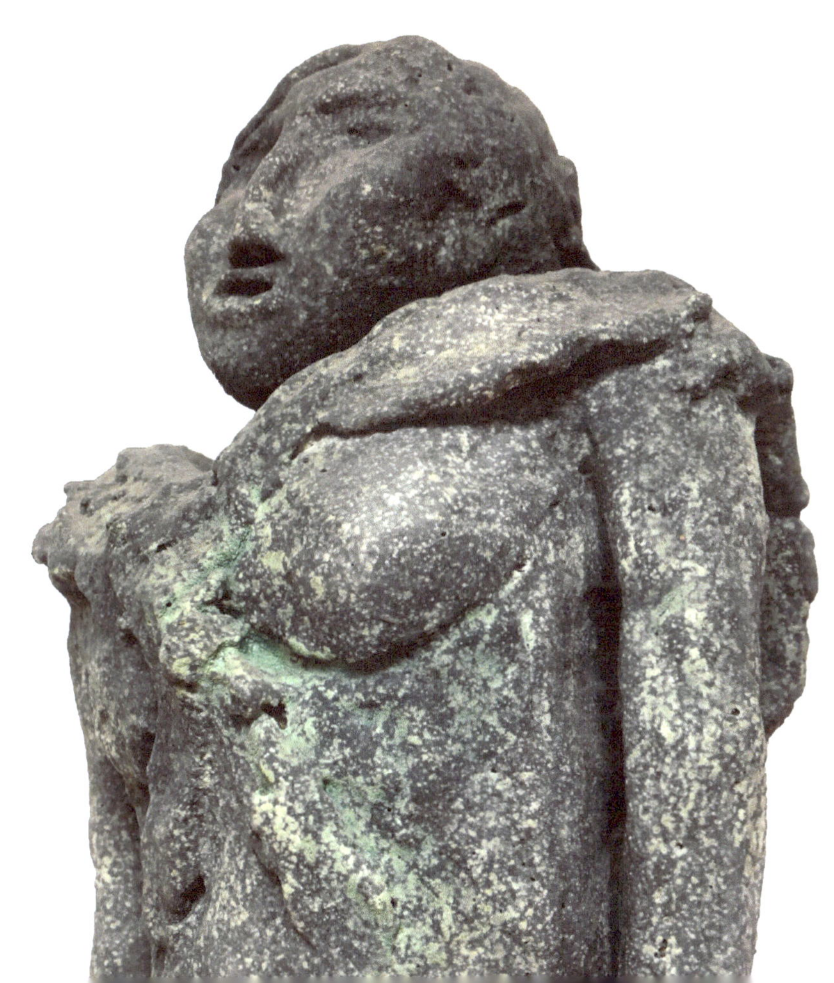

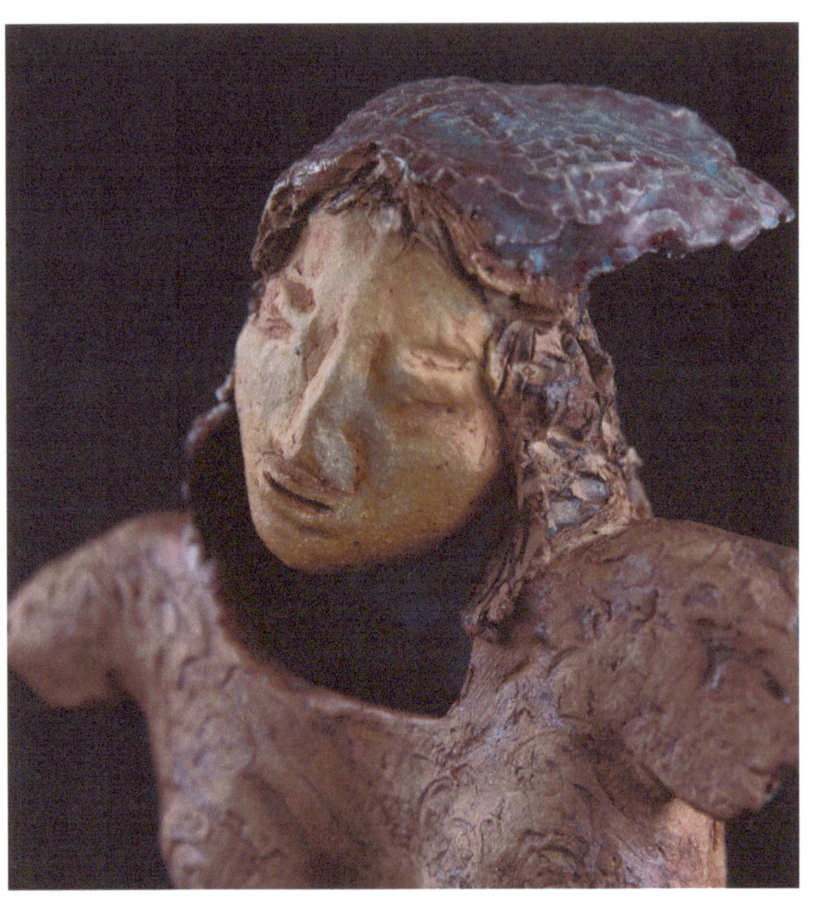

A snake is sunning
still as death.
Birds move from roof to pole.
The boy cradles a paper boat
searches the ocean.
A plate of bread, tomato
wait on the grass.
The gate open.
The gate open.

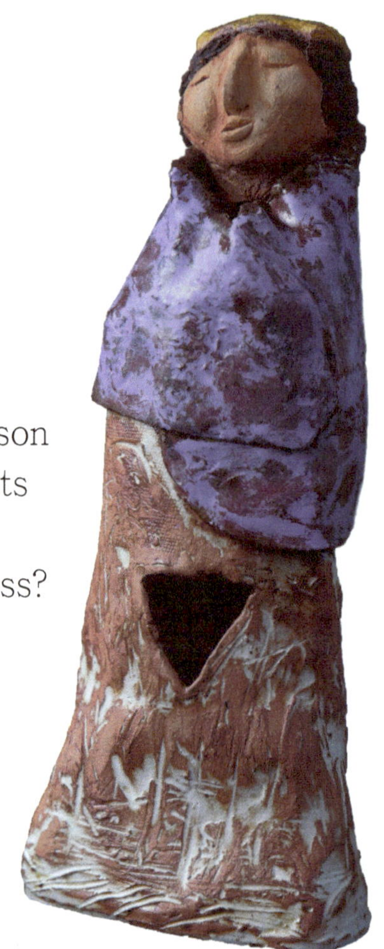

Does every season
have its bequests
symphony
anatomy of a kiss?

This day is forgetting
remembrance
the sun leaps then pilfers
the rain withholds
then floods
the summer bride
apostrophes winter
hummingbirds feast
on the feeder's nectar
their tiny bodies
tethered to faith.

In
the
Country
of
Sorrows

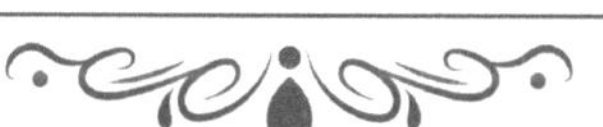

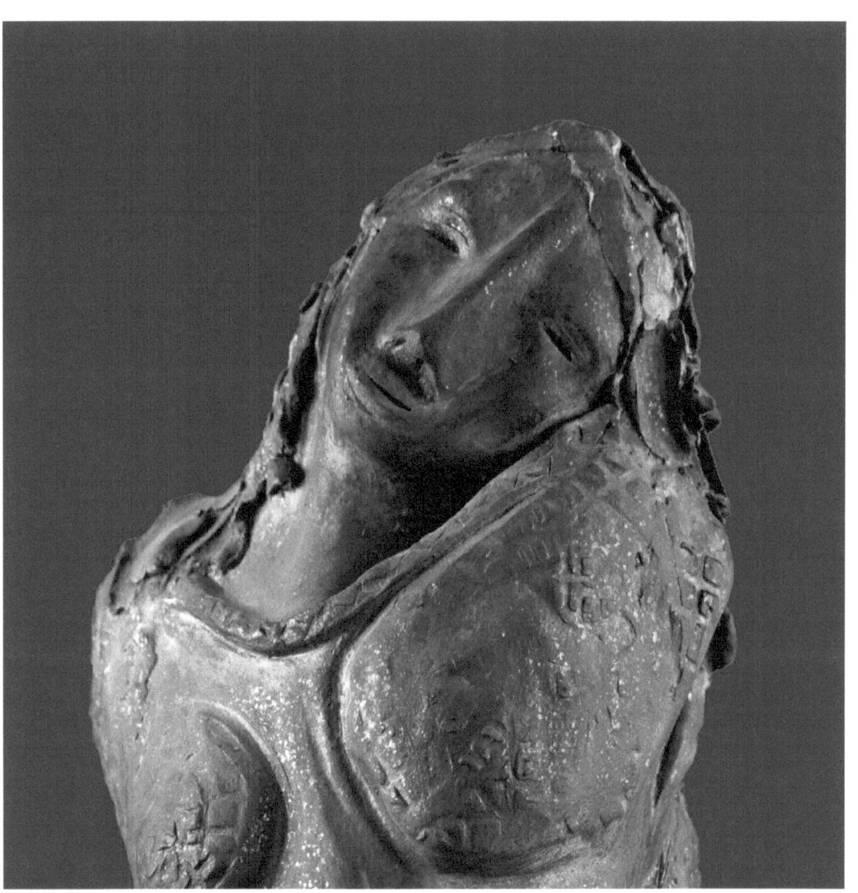

To climb your stars
I wore my elevator shoes
but still the night spoke distance
stole crocus
my meager seed
turned frost.

As a child I spoke to the wind
curved my words
around poem and petal
pantomine and prelude.
But the tides broke loose
the night knit my brow
to the country of sorrows.

To reach the sky
I wore my winged coat
promised to stay faithful
but the floods came
and the wind
the wind.

How will I conquer might
with the power
of my twig sticks?

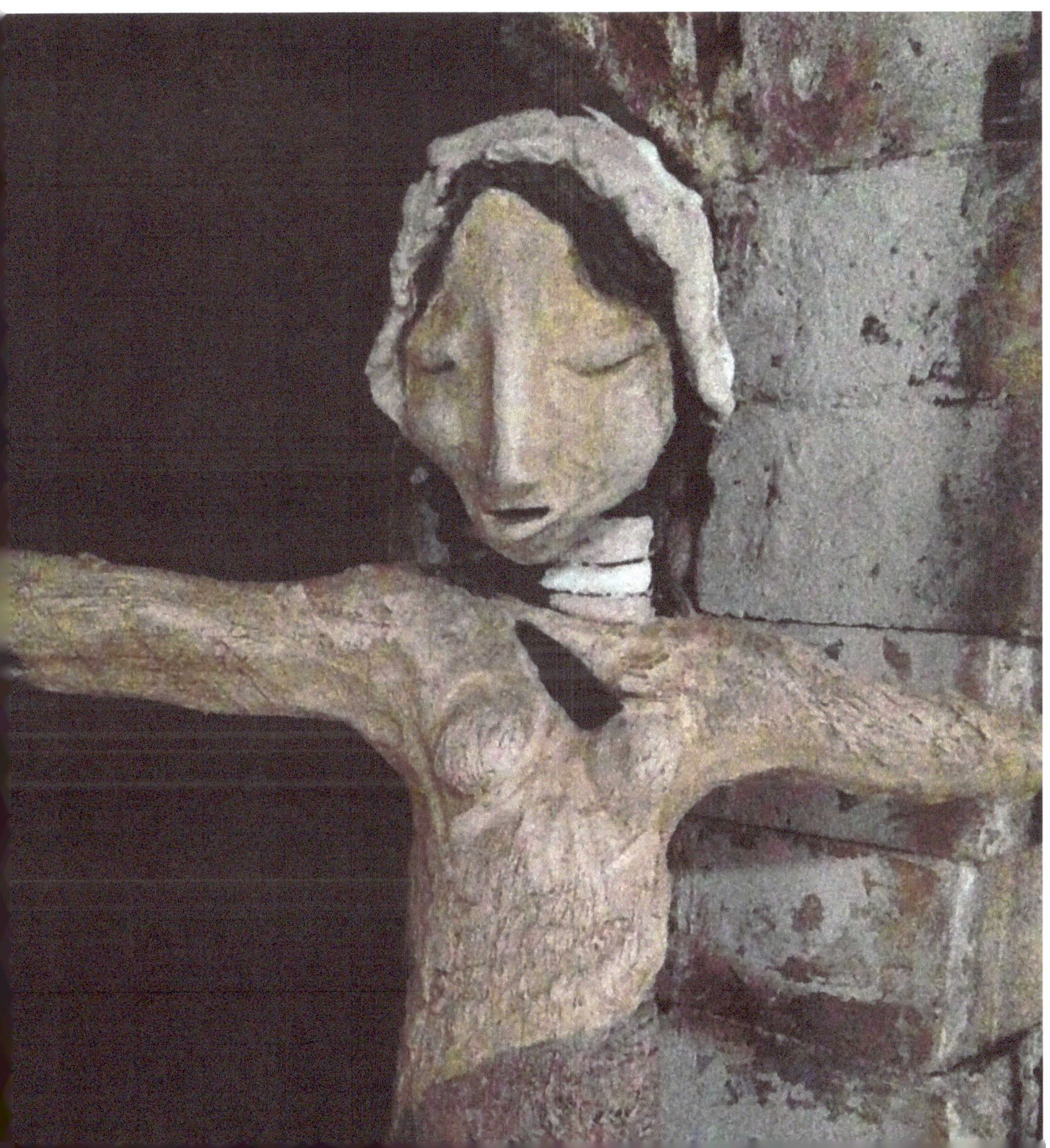

My sight hinders me.
Words are a palm of oil
in a slippery landscape.
How will I enter your hem
sleep there?

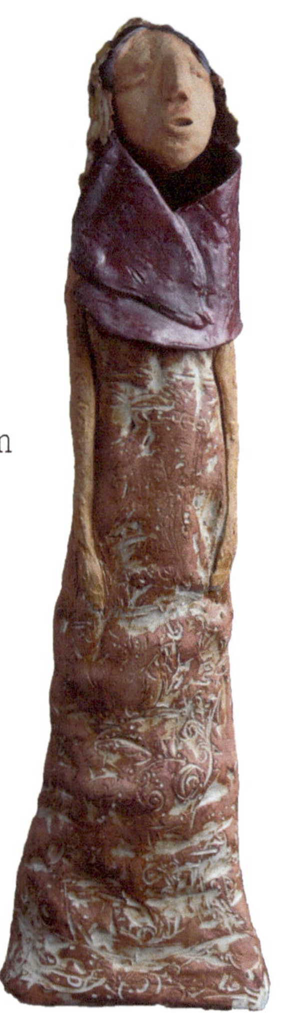

Let me sing
not out of lack
but out of seed.

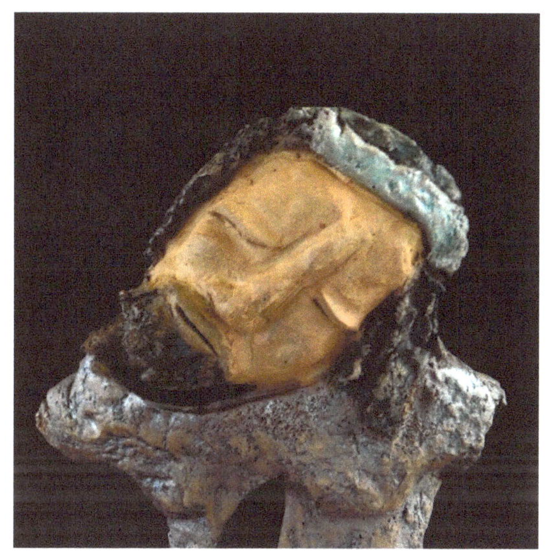

Can we walk hand in hand
even if sometimes I limp
a shy creature
in the land of giants?

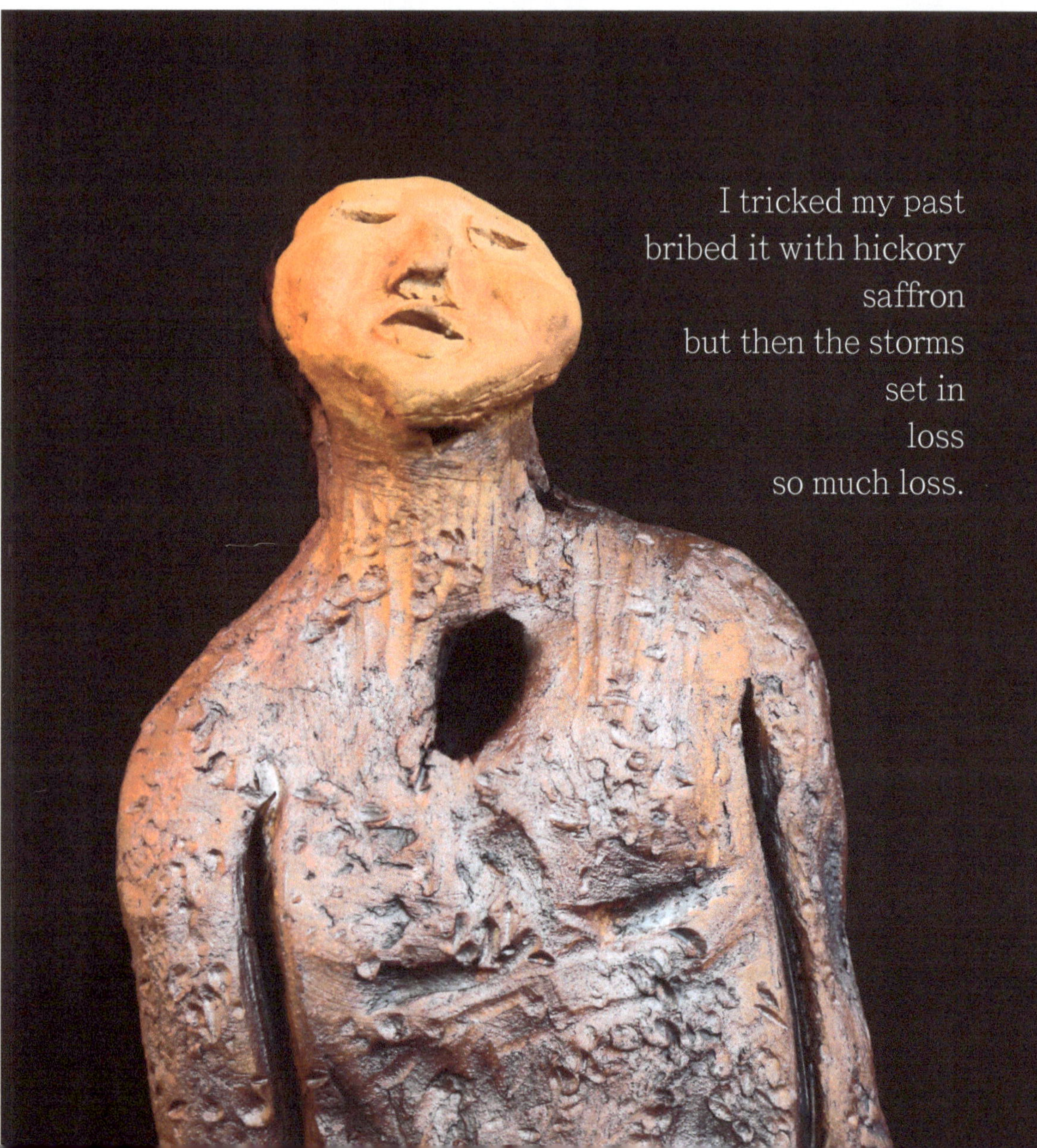

I tricked my past
bribed it with hickory
saffron
but then the storms
set in
loss
so much loss.

What wages war
jangles my soul
makes for holes
in the upholstery
the mechanical dog
with the lost key?

You speak with the dead
burnish their headstones
cut the dark loose
carry my stories
not as burden or conceit.

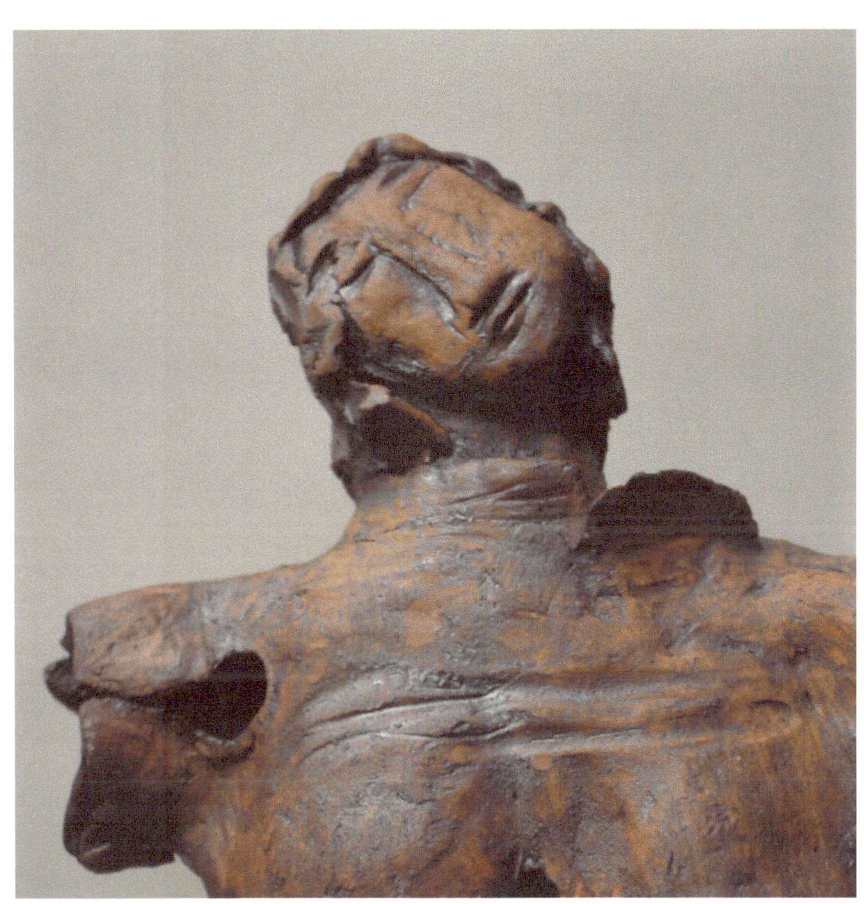

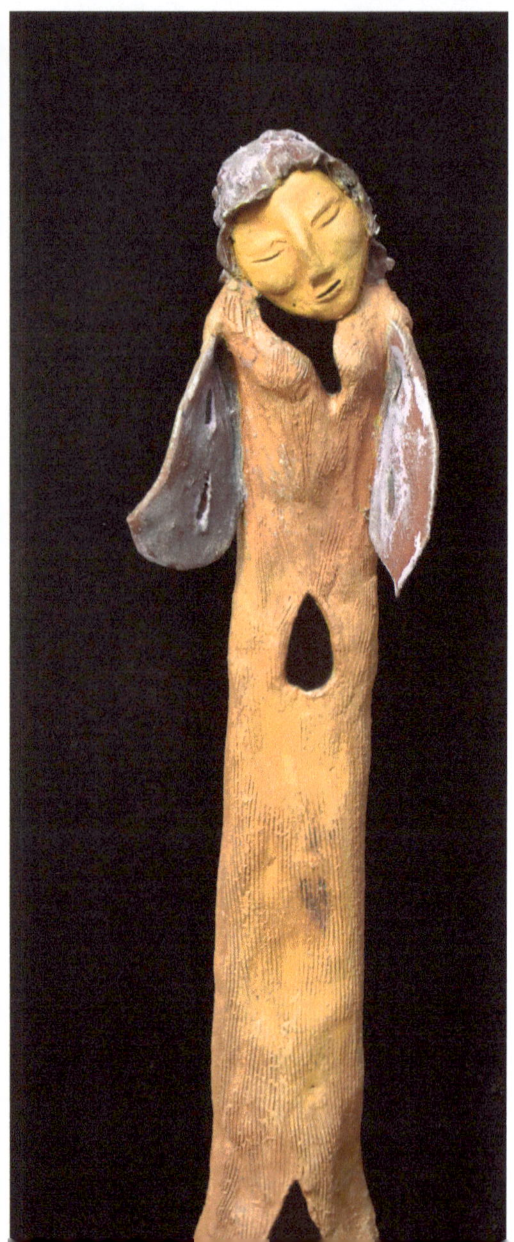

I travel a land
of dim light
fairies
fish
so many fish.

In the sea of merchants
who will unbind
the dark's bramble
call us to a different
measure of feast?

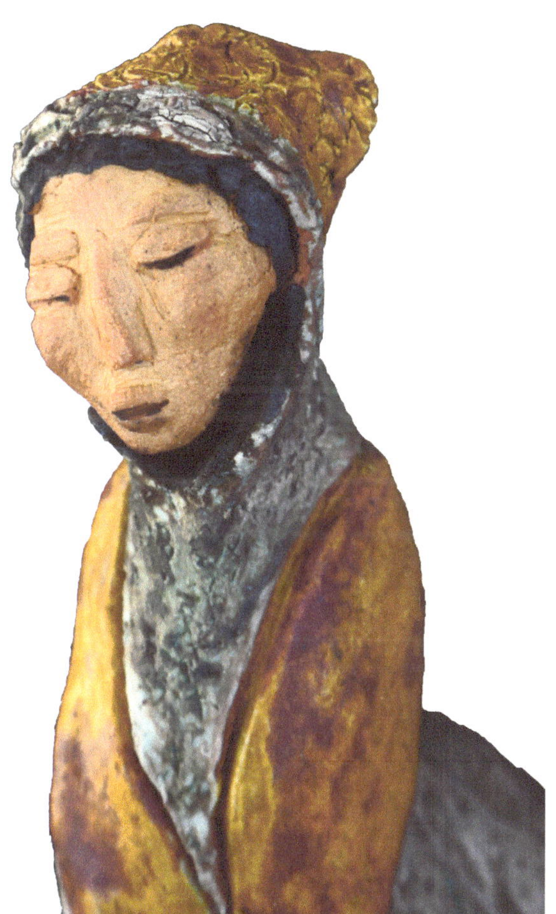

How many inquisitions
fallen houses?
When the face of
the stranger comes
I do not want to be afraid.

If I could appease you with lilac
a buttonhole's carnation
would my days come right
a seat appear
at the dark's feast table?

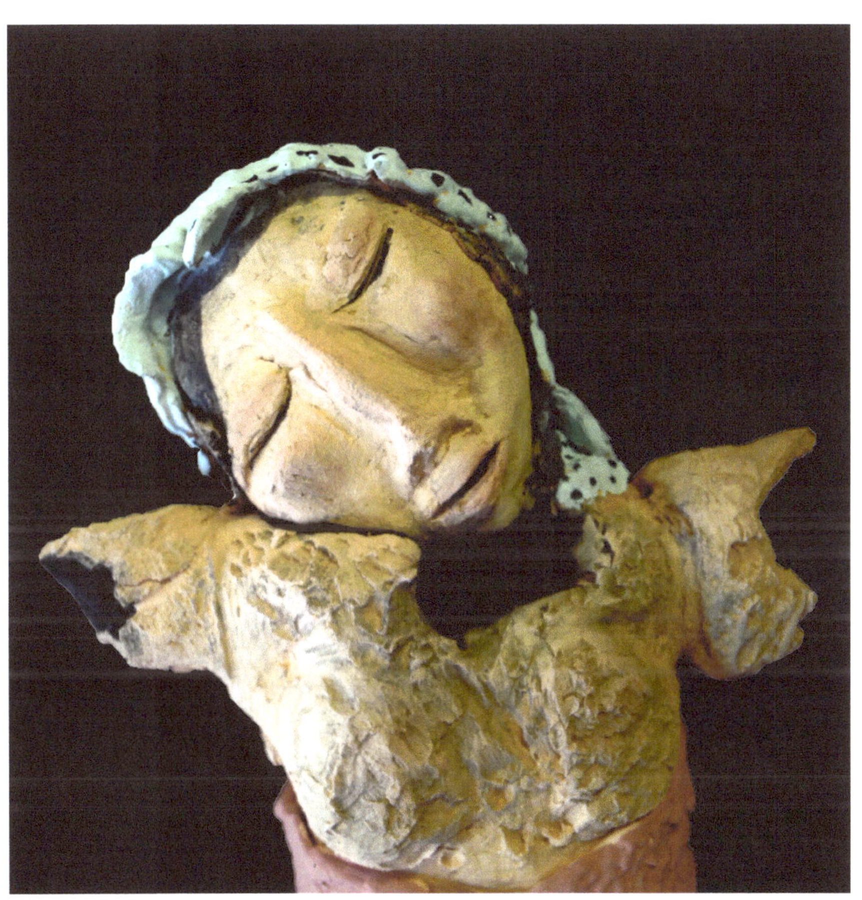

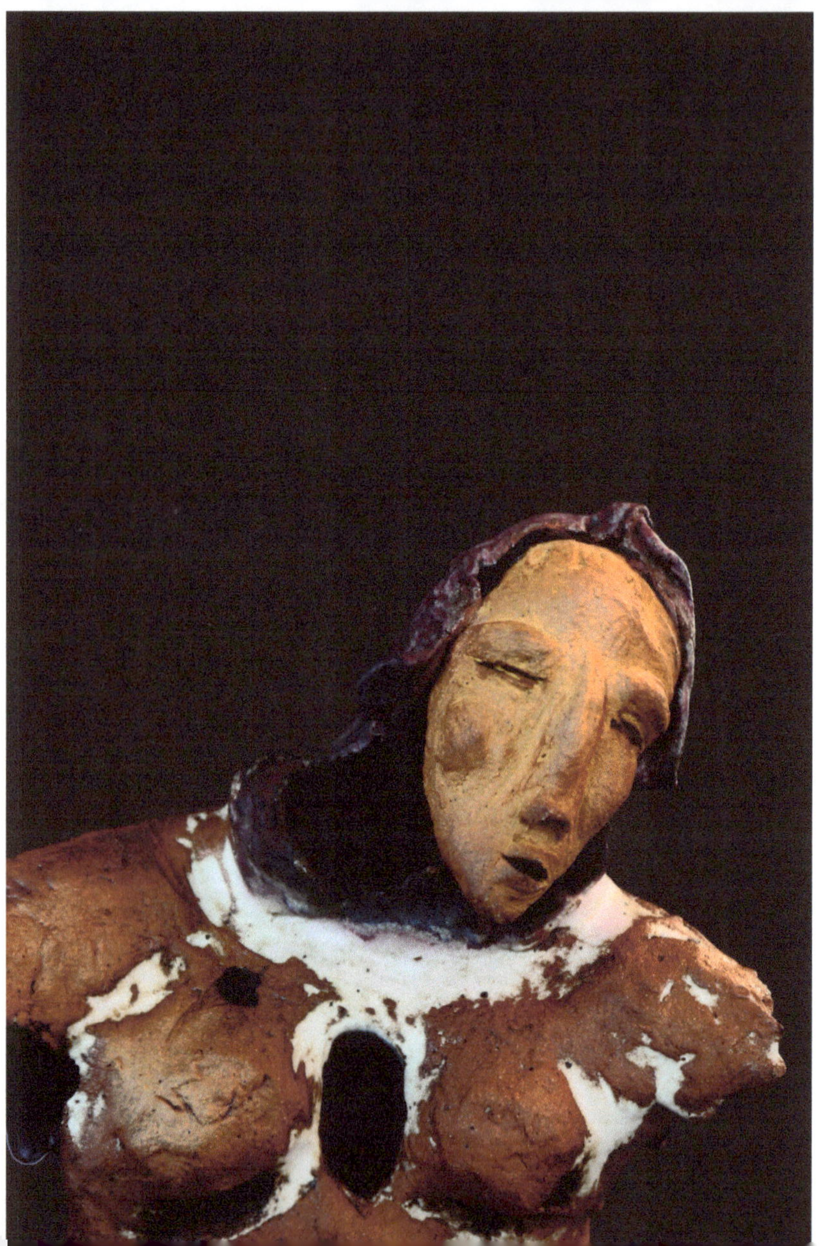

When you call my name
out of the wormed wood
calamities
will I come to you
pale as the sunken reed
or rose tinged
about to be born?

Let me not live in an
over dusted house
where fictions breed
the day turns peephole.

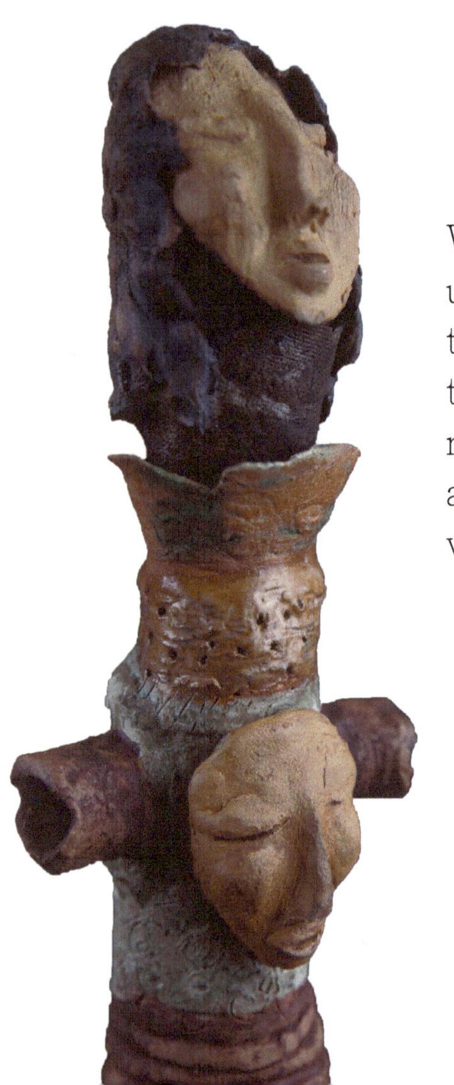

What if the night
unsullies my past
turns me into more than
the blind eye
ravenous bird
arrives
with a pear tree?

Even in the stymied moments
when the sun didn't know me
the sky was a bruised sister
I waited for the dust to lift
your voice to enter.

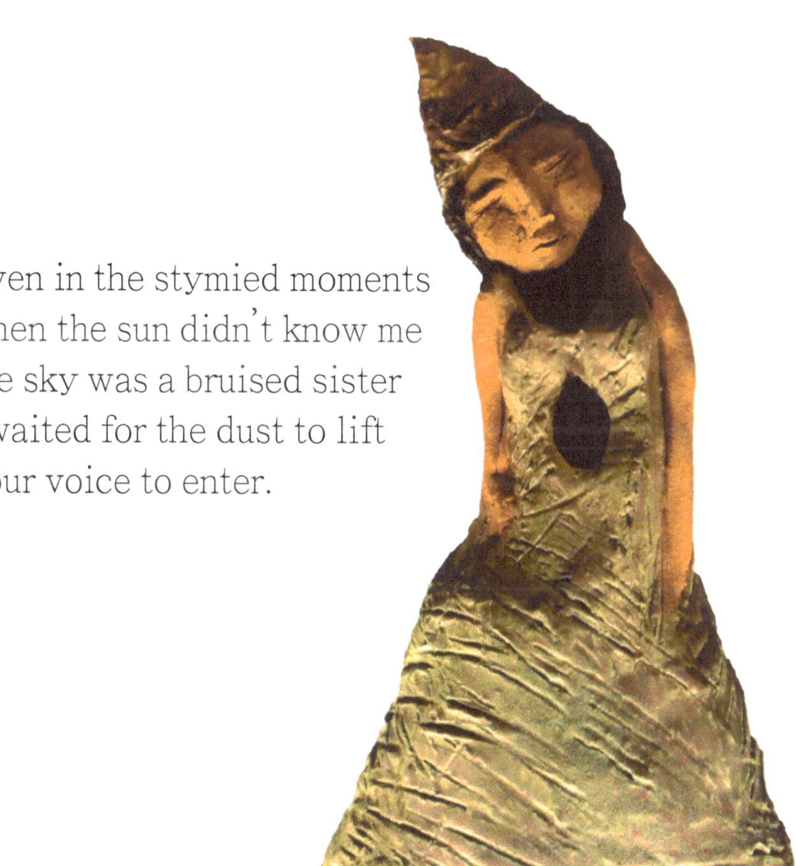

How will I come to you?
Lemon yellow
with my life
burning?

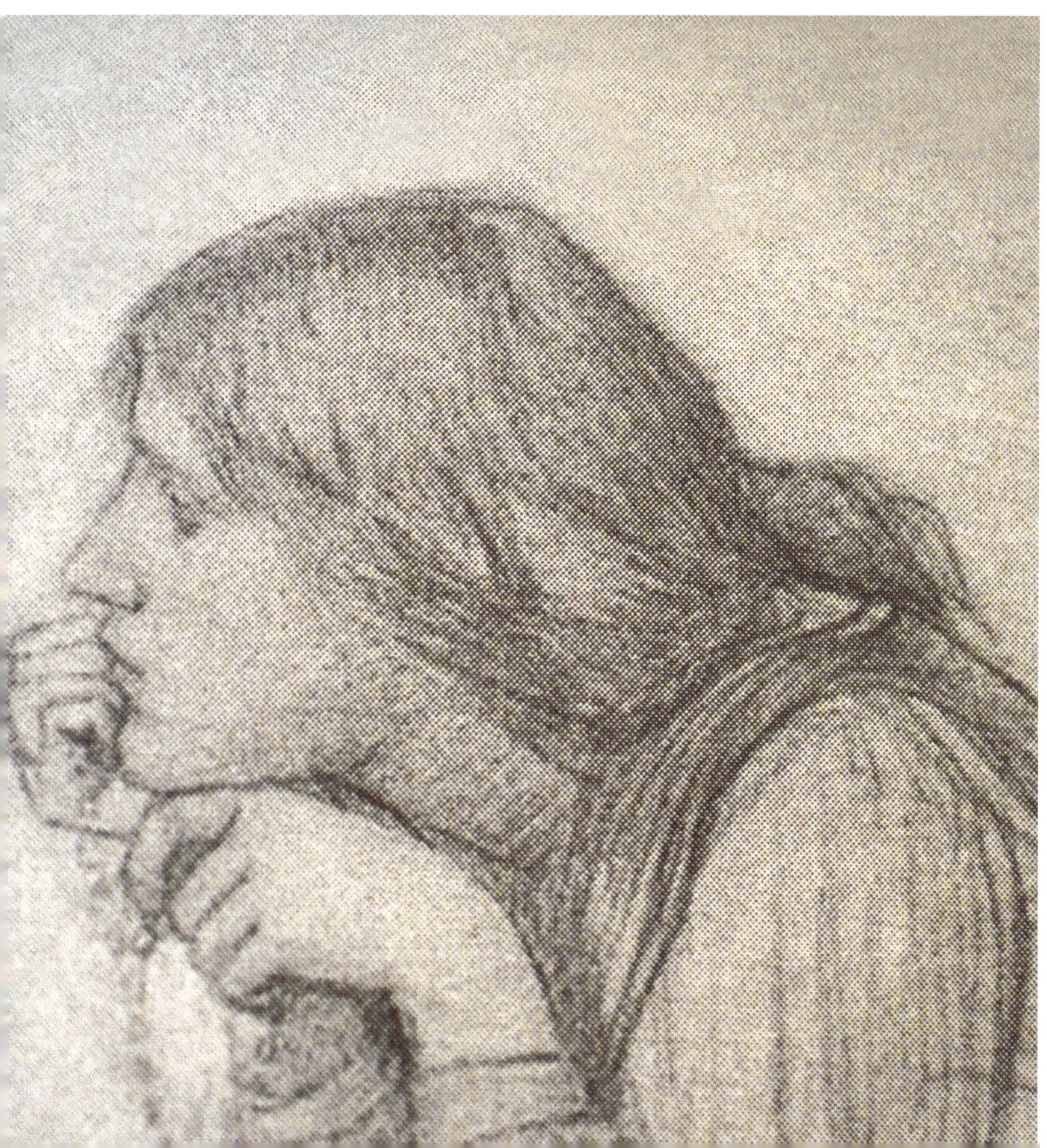

Wild
and
Spinning

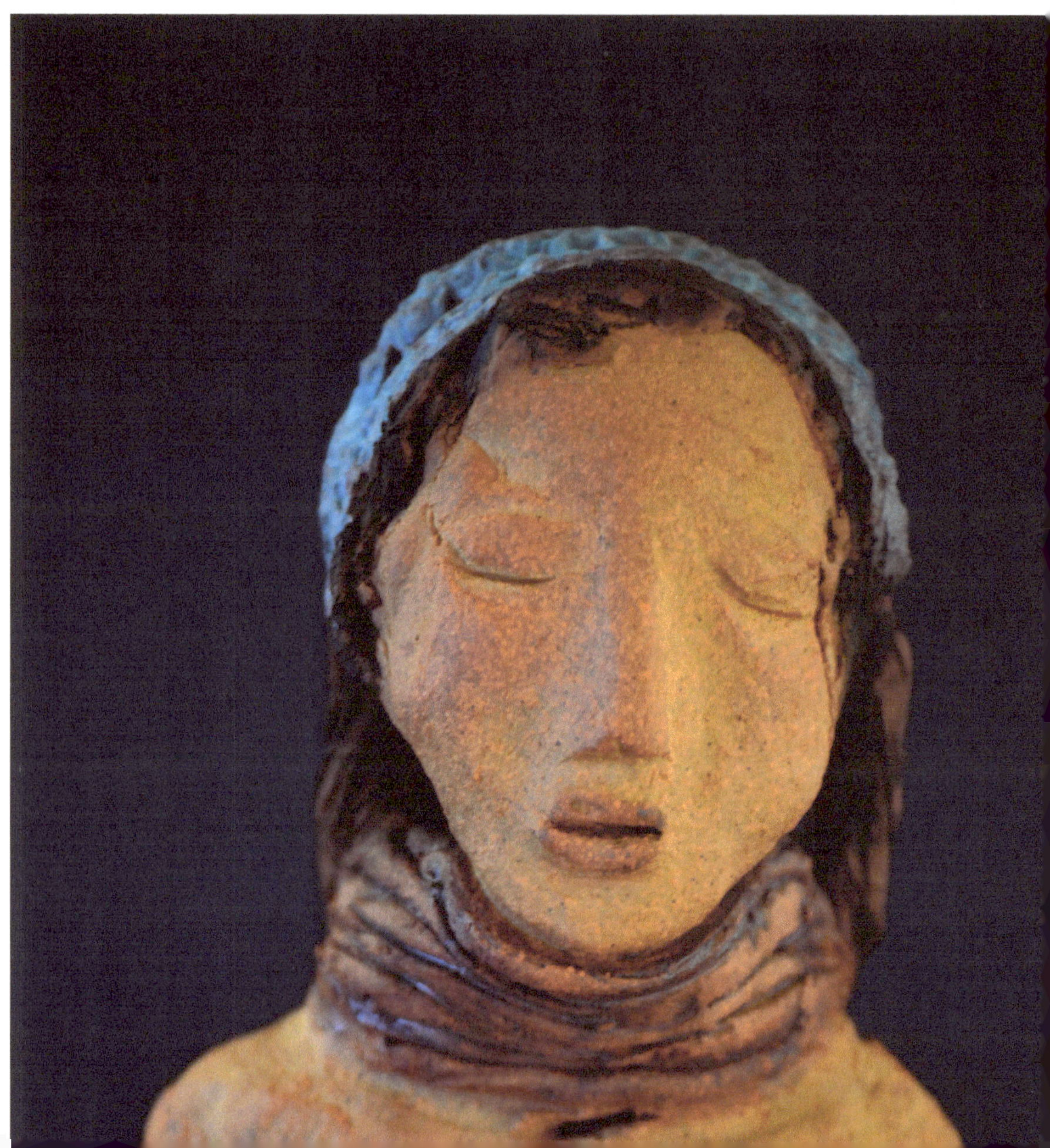

The night was shrouded
with fog, hearsay
but the moon refused to bow
to the dark's imperialism.

In my heart
star after star after star
wild and spinning.

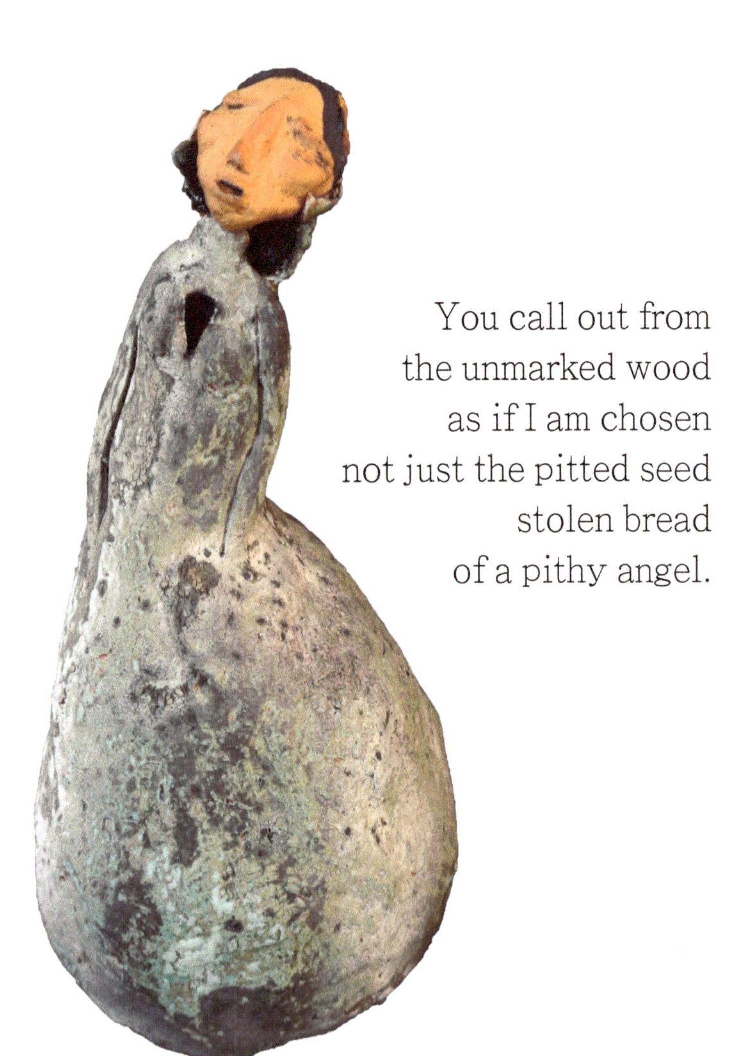

You call out from
the unmarked wood
as if I am chosen
not just the pitted seed
stolen bread
of a pithy angel.

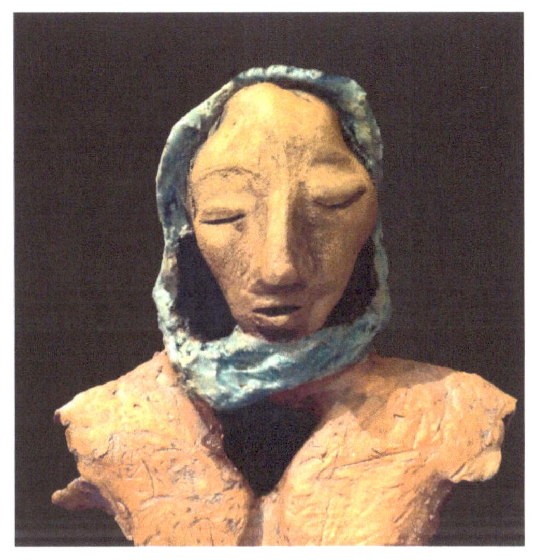

You disrobe the past
rummage the cargo trunk
of my heart's displeasures.

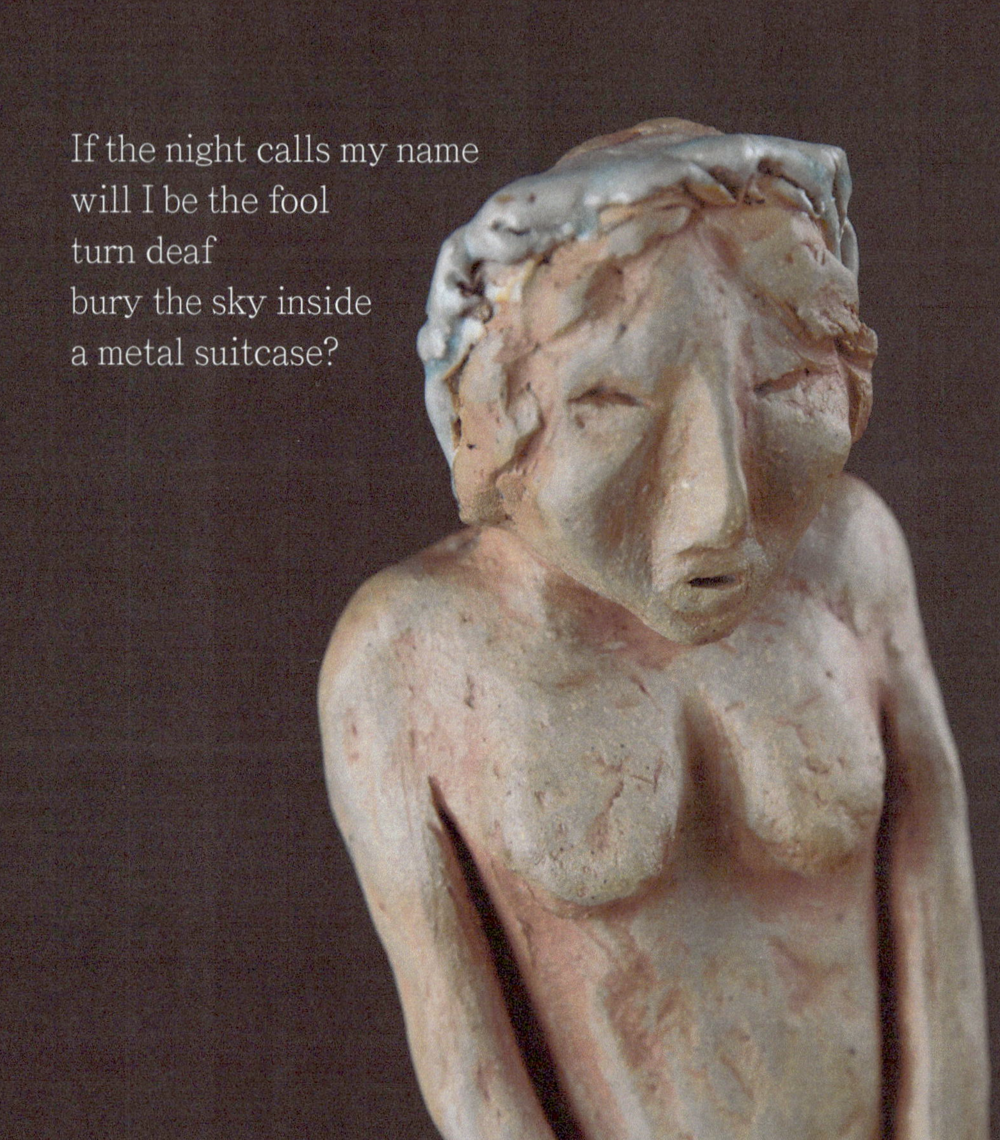
If the night calls my name
will I be the fool
turn deaf
bury the sky inside
a metal suitcase?

I want to woo you
with poems
diligence
soup and latkes
care packages
salt.

I let the shy one in
who nurses wounded animals
anoints the poor woman's table
with fish.

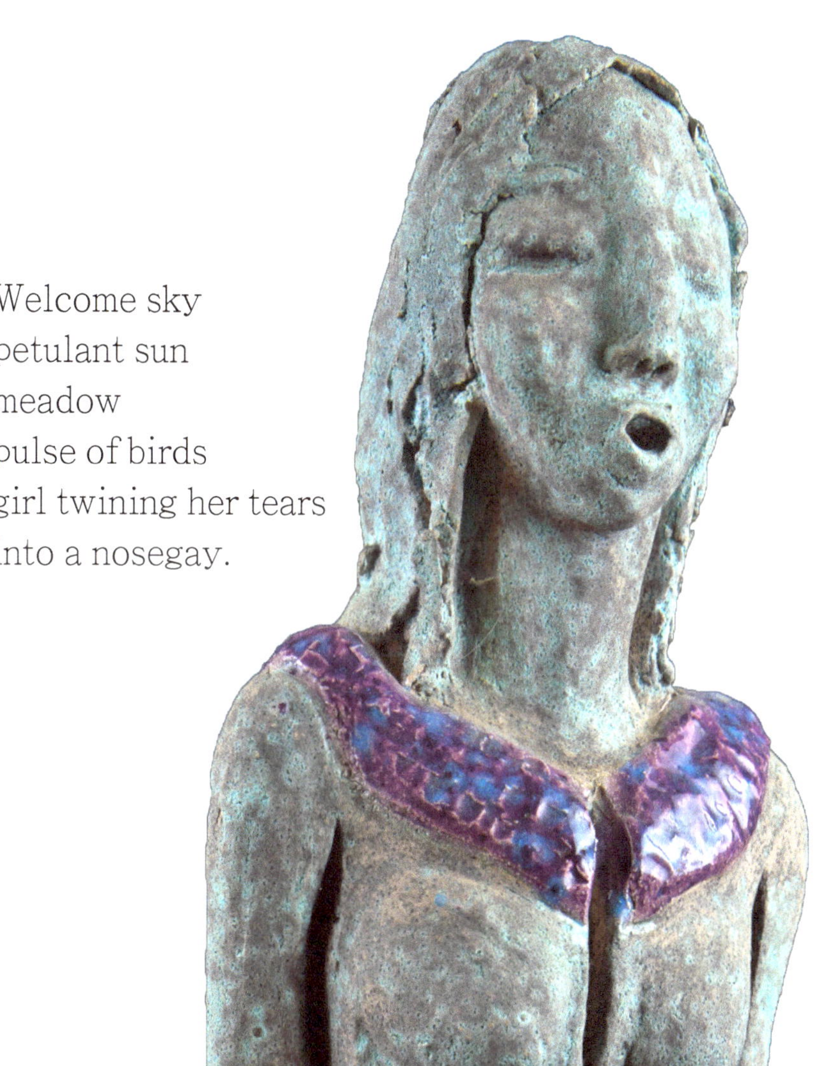

Welcome sky
petulant sun
meadow
pulse of birds
girl twining her tears
into a nosegay.

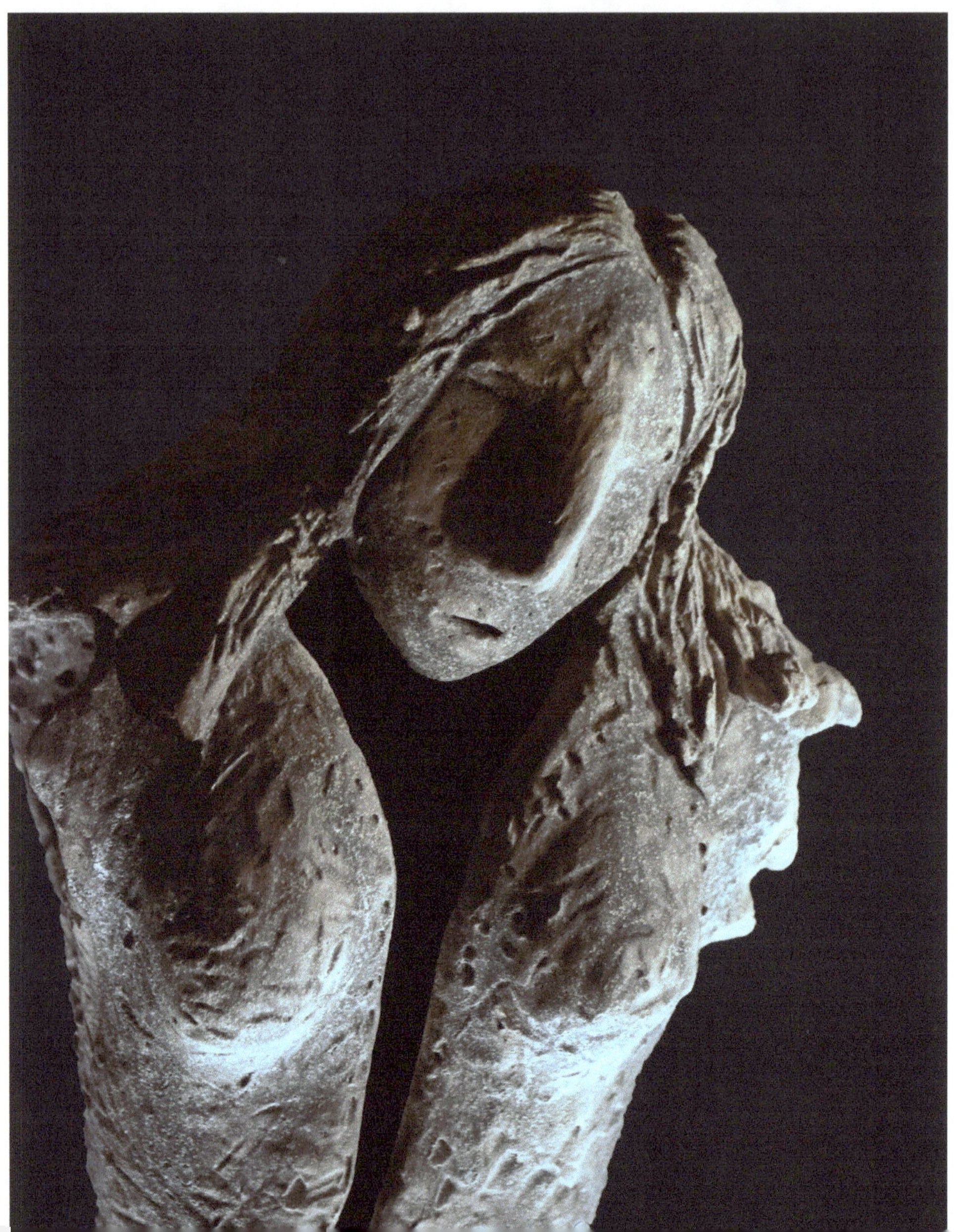

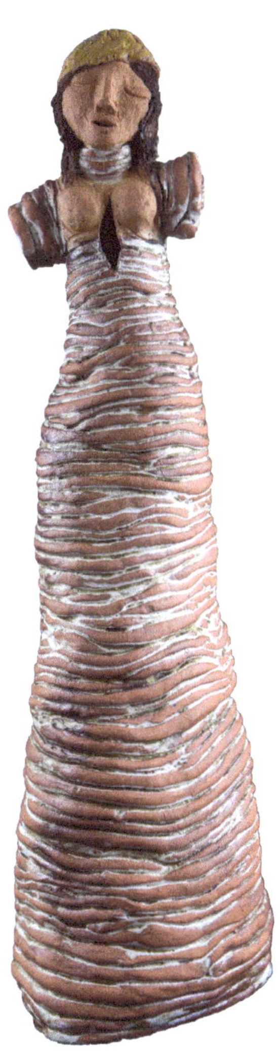

Every act of faith
fevers me
with longing and flame
carries me to places
I never planned to go.

How can I explain
my seriousness
the years wasted
way you stir snow
amongst the willows
rise up in the tree
as verse?

When I rehearse death
give it a good talking to
will lament call my name
the forgotten girl rise up
speak the language of doves?

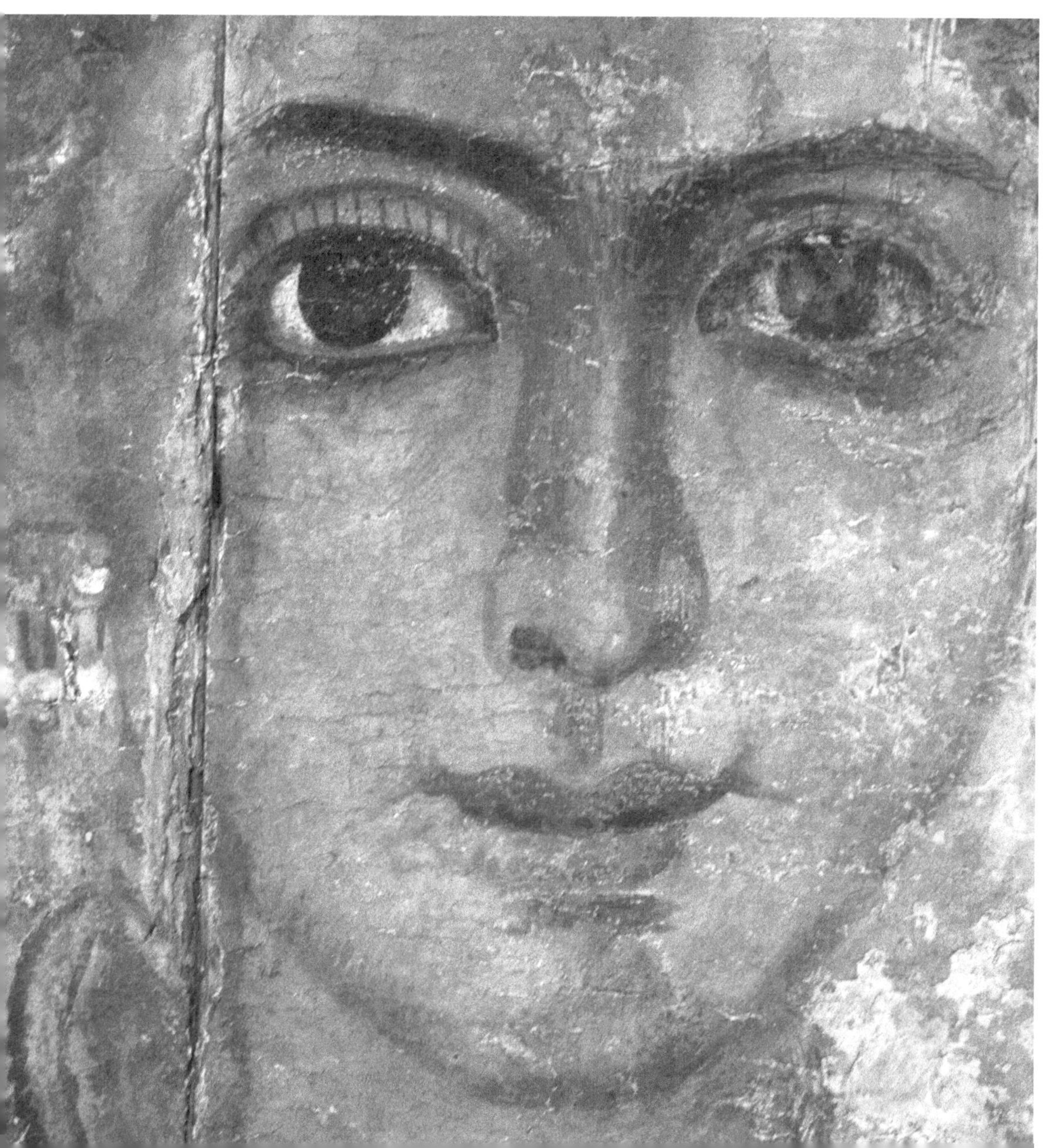

The night traffics in fireflies
a mysterious wind.
If I'm going to come
I better come naked
silent
unabused.

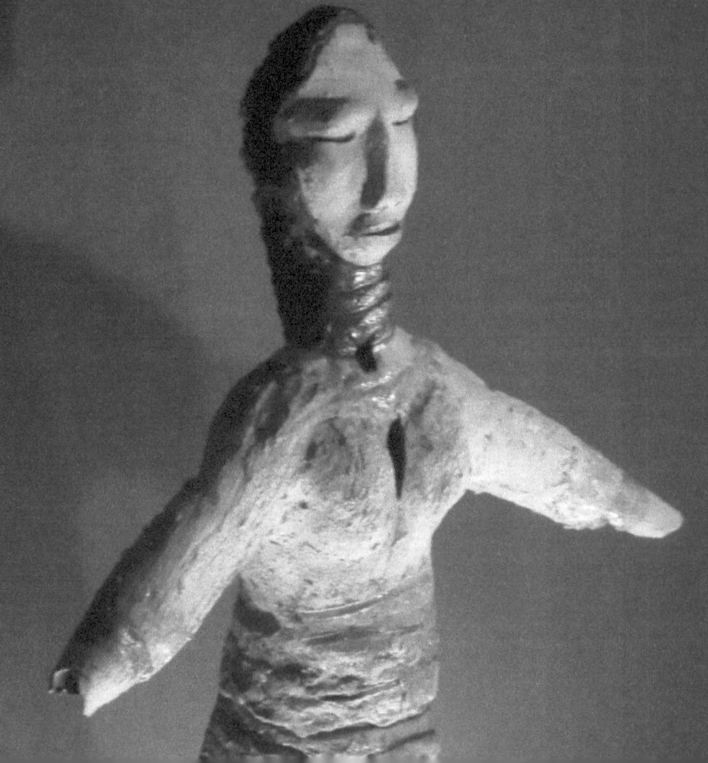

Your beacon serpents the dark
carries the boat to safety
unbinds the man
fastens my shoes
to the sky's dance floor.

To kiss the hem
of your garment
I unbury my sled
dust my voice
of its icicles.

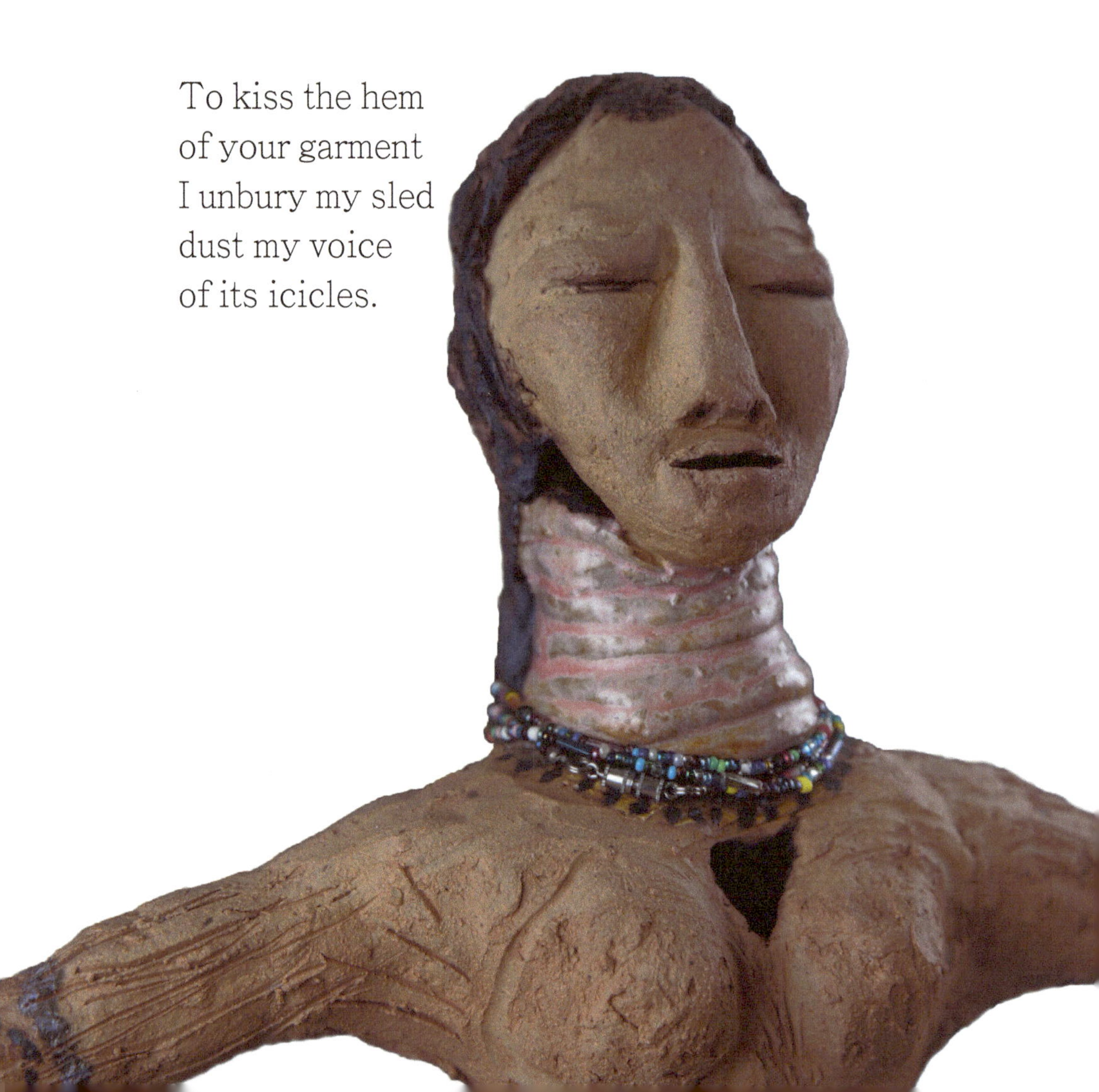

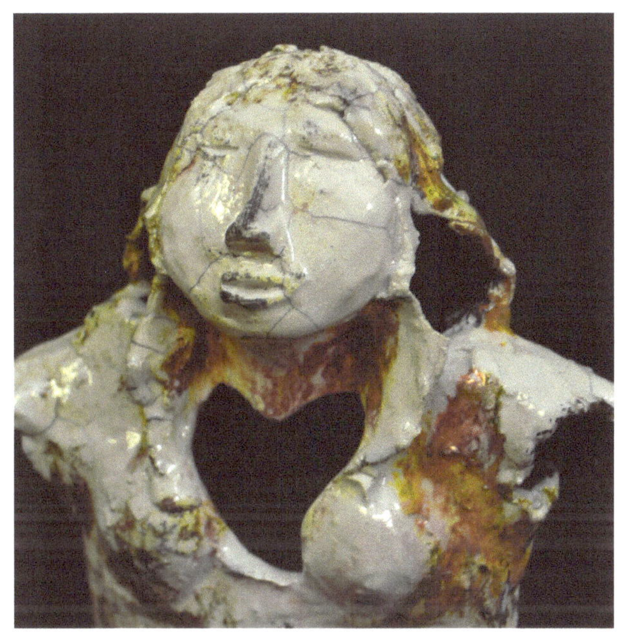

You slip in
rummage.
Ice falls from the trees.
My condemned past
grows a meadow.

You shore up
my weary voice
move past pretense
to feast table
the dancing iris
in a silken dress.

To bathe in the land
of your kisses
I unbind my hair
become birdwing
bog.

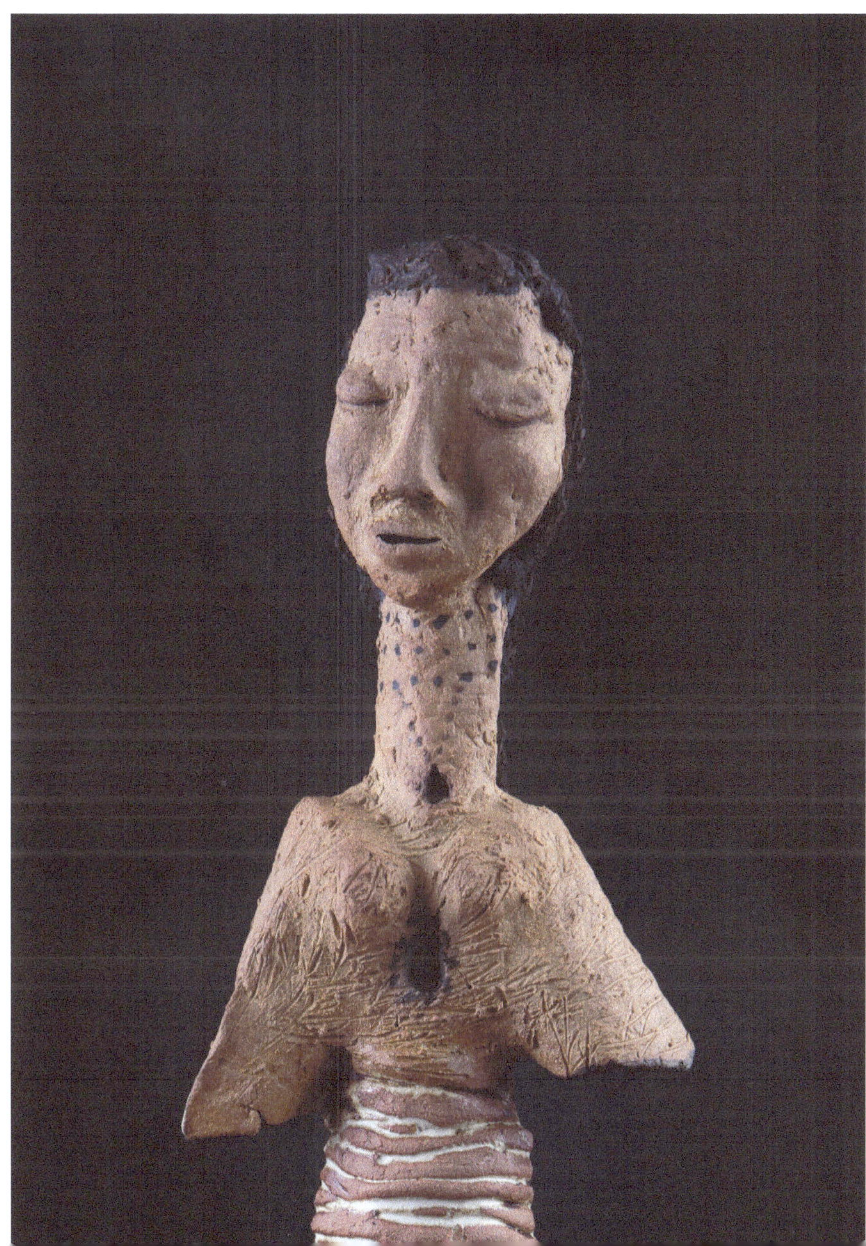

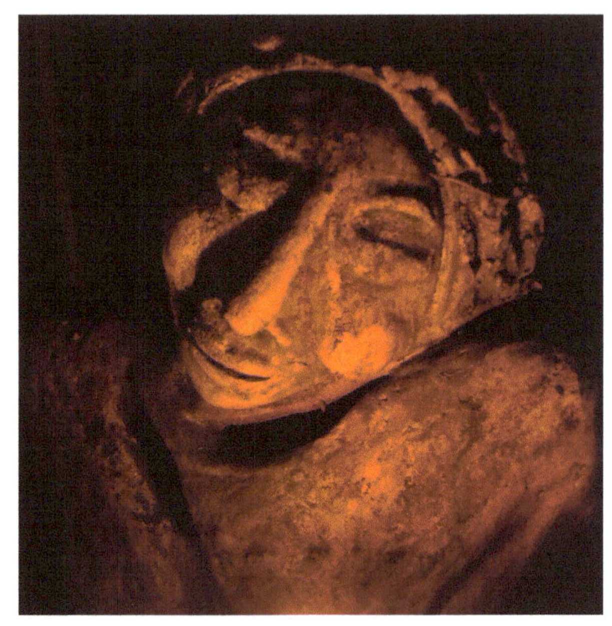

I have saved
the red tinged holly
plump figs
from the old country
unfasten my robes.

You call till the wolf flees
the night disavows weapons
my voice becomes spindle and thread.
The stars, the stars
splash my dress
with a sea of dew.

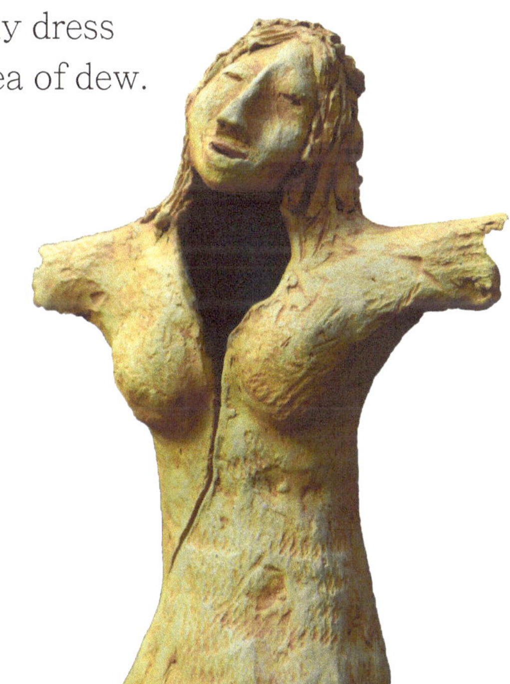

You
Unravel
Me

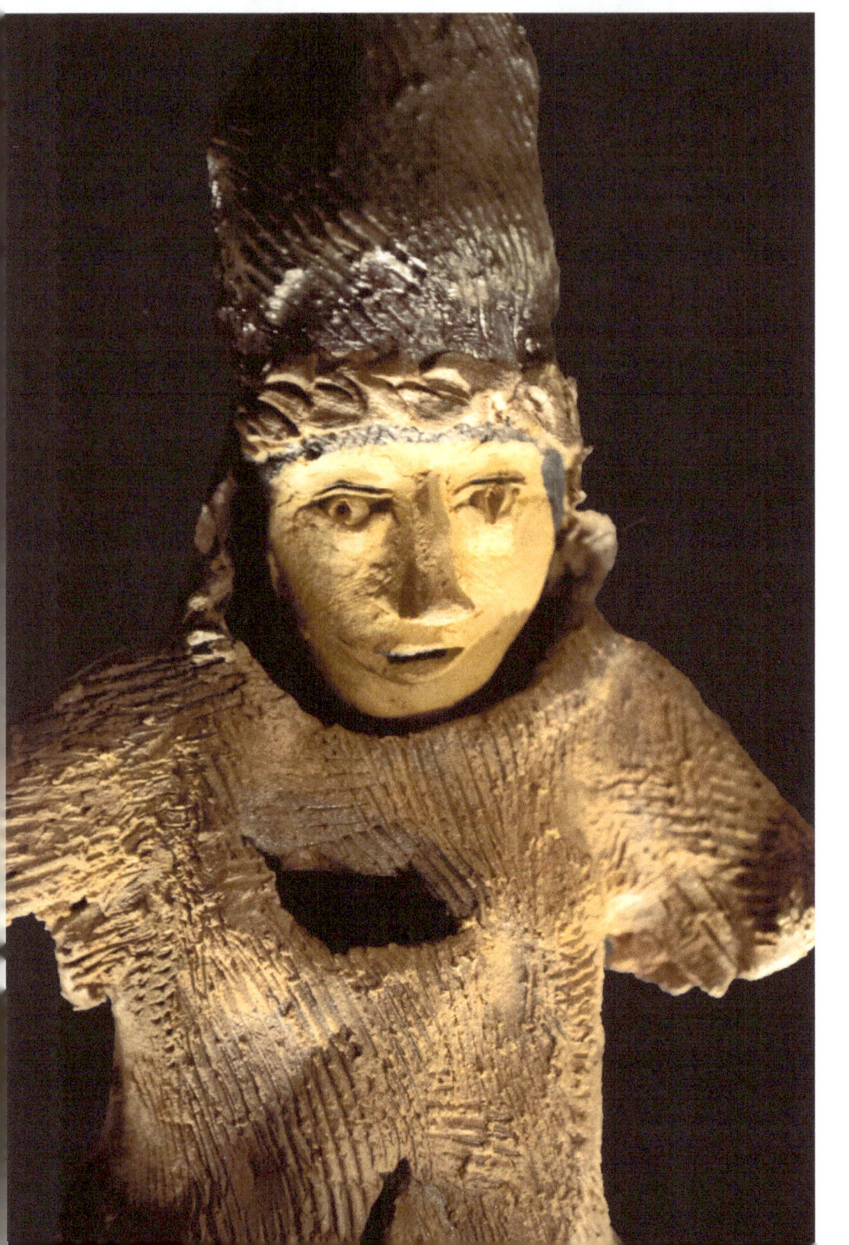

The sky is a black fist
the field monograms locust.
You call to me
I slip into my morning coat
remember.

                              No nuptial with death
                              derails me
                              now that my wants have fled
                              snow envelops the meadow.

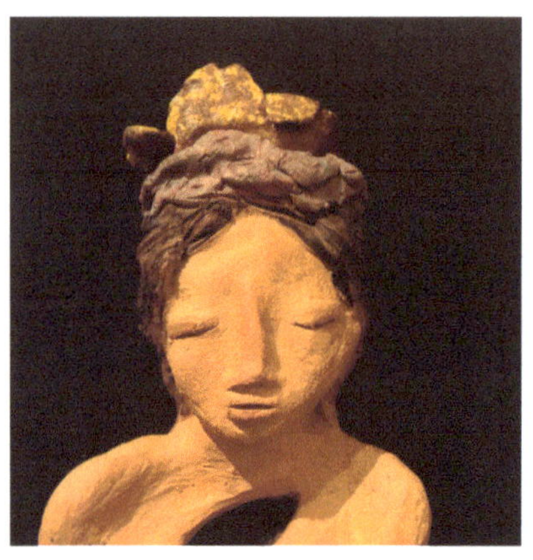

I sweep the ocean
tame galaxies
burnish death
till my dreams
grow a pear tree.

To refind my ancient shoes
I court willow and brook
peony and meadow
children, many children
the sea that floods
the sea that empties.

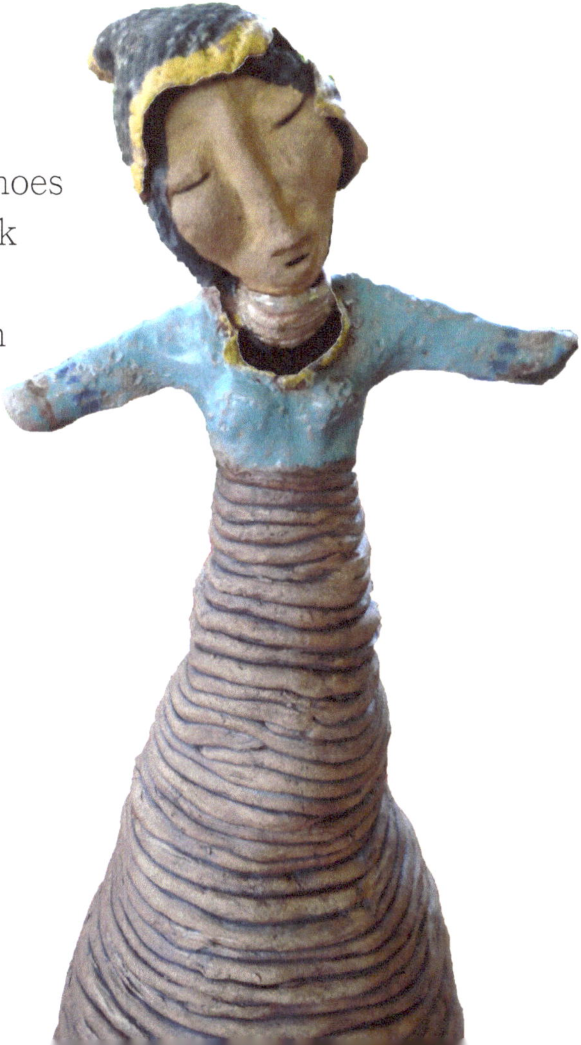

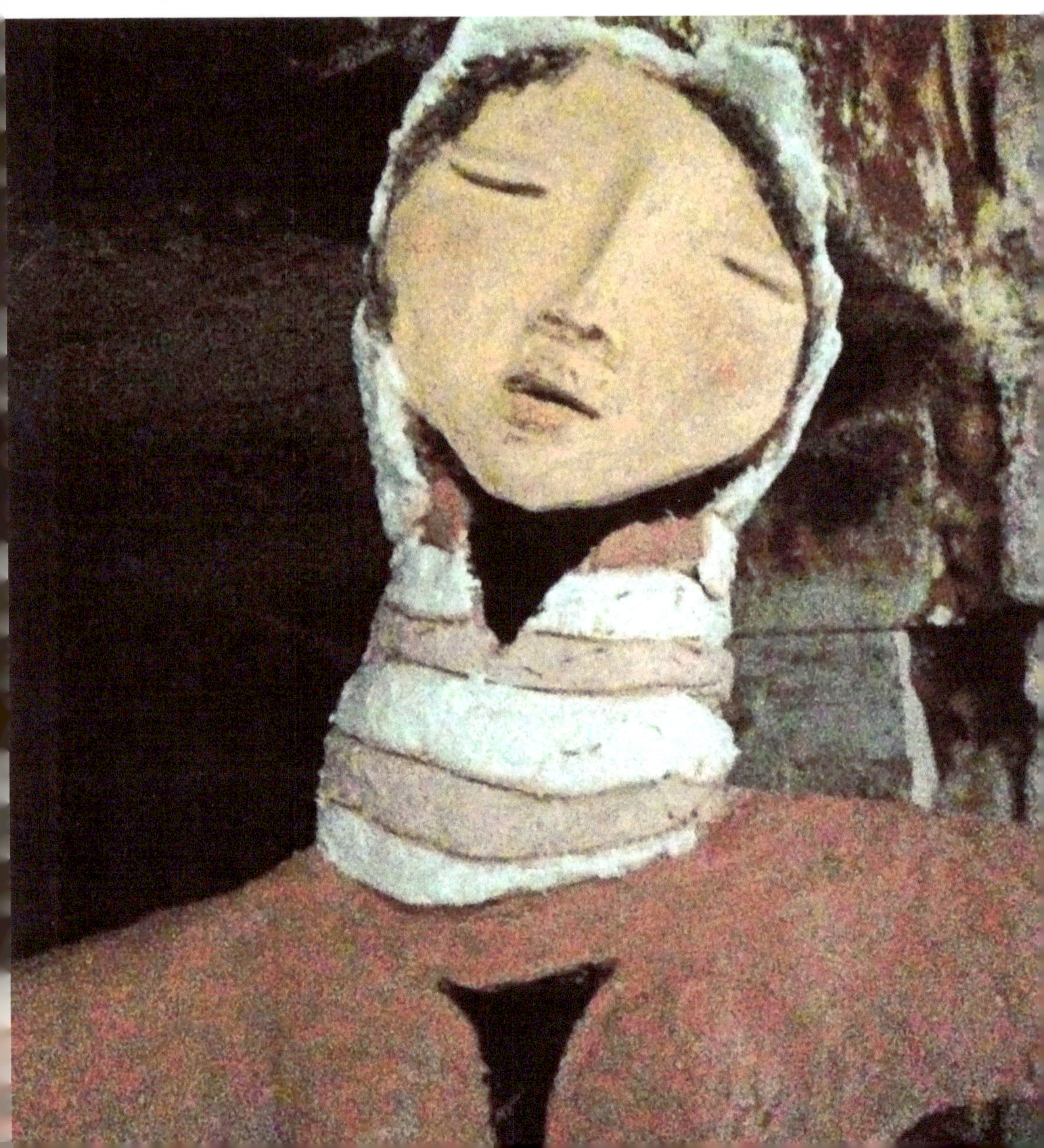

The barn door unhinged
by the wind's fury
still flowers persist
song drifts
I slide into my coral coat.

There is nothing I need
accomplish
to drown in your love.

Be still
I tell myself
and pomegranates
prosper the field
the sky offers up scarlet
birds waltz
tree to tree to tree.

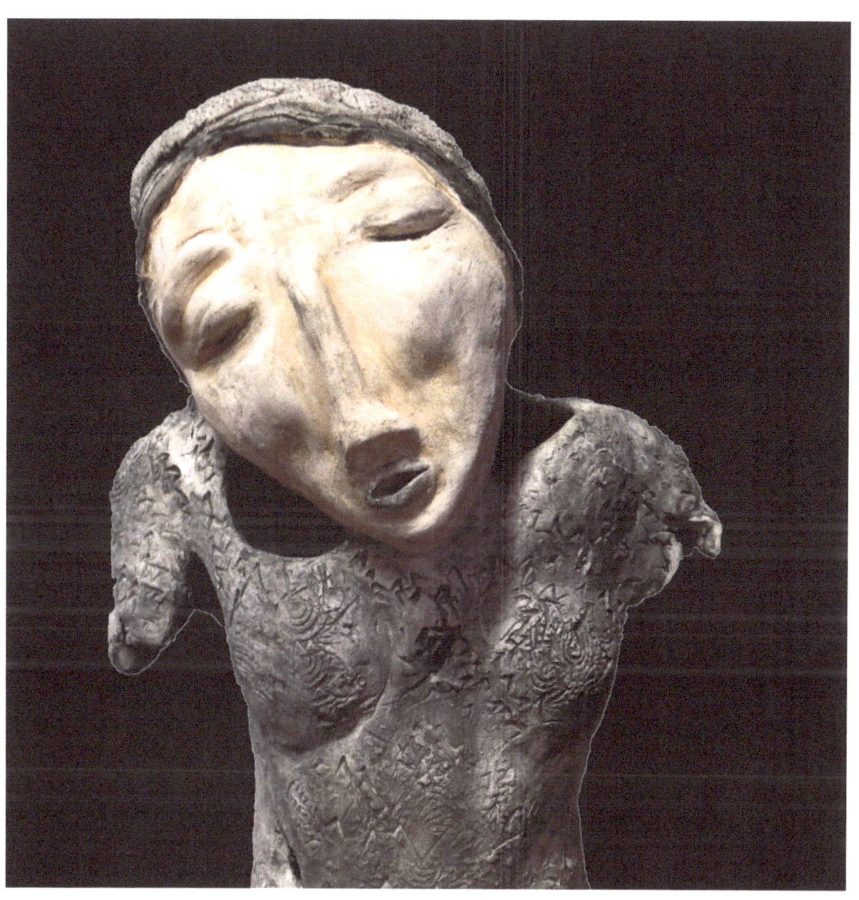

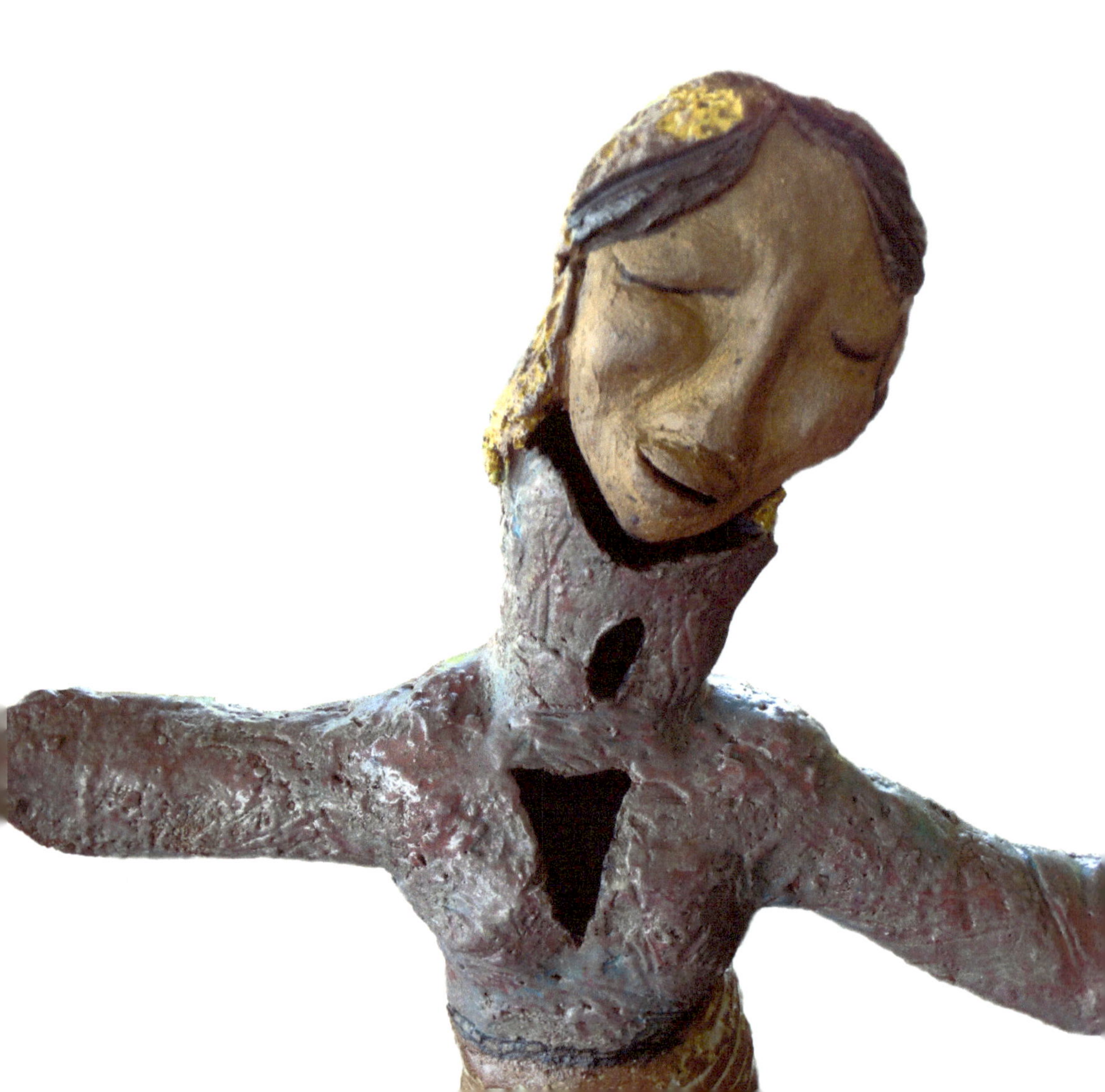

I no longer pinch words
force them to soldier
now that the night
carries no curse
my shoes are a burning bush
every waltz
traffics with you.

Like the fevered moth
I cleave to your lamp's totem
let the light eat me.

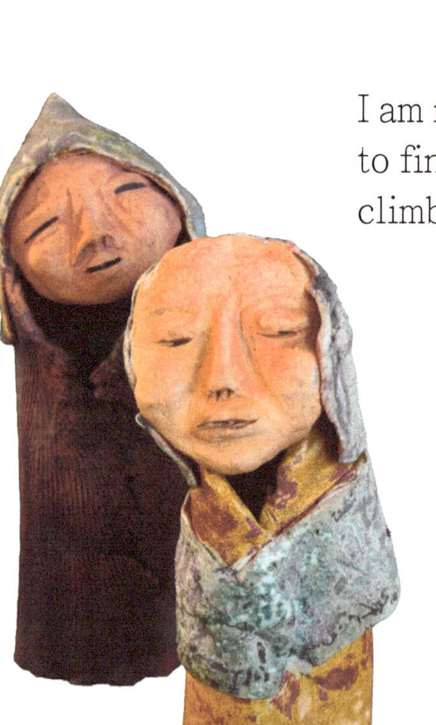

I am not afraid
to find strange creatures
climbing about my branches.

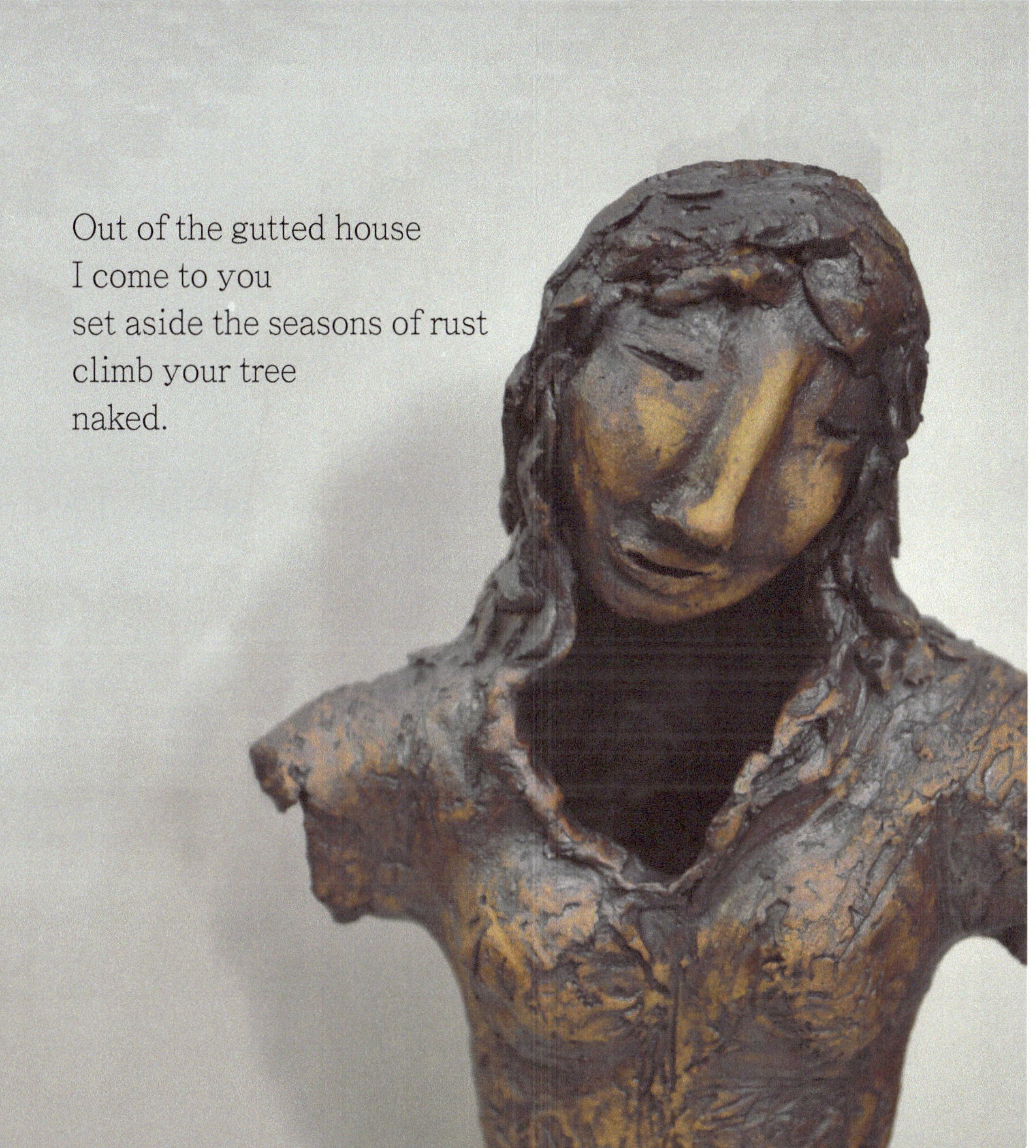
Out of the gutted house
I come to you
set aside the seasons of rust
climb your tree
naked.

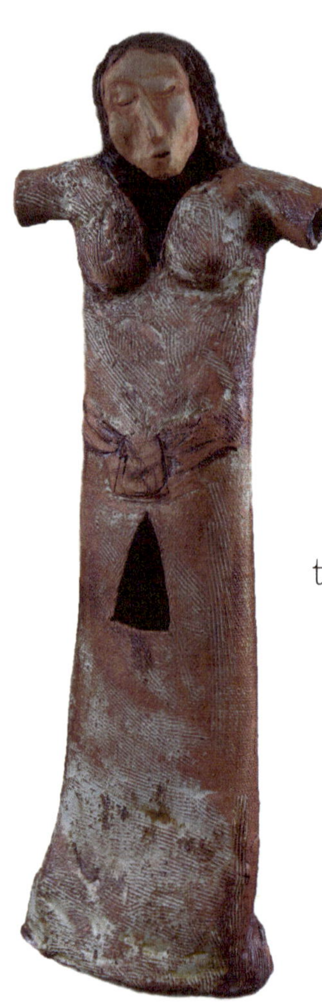

The pallbearer of lost things
I walk the path of stones
bake bread
call morning out
of her nightshirt
watch seasons slip away
the birds return to their nest eggs.

You conquer everything.
You conquer everything.

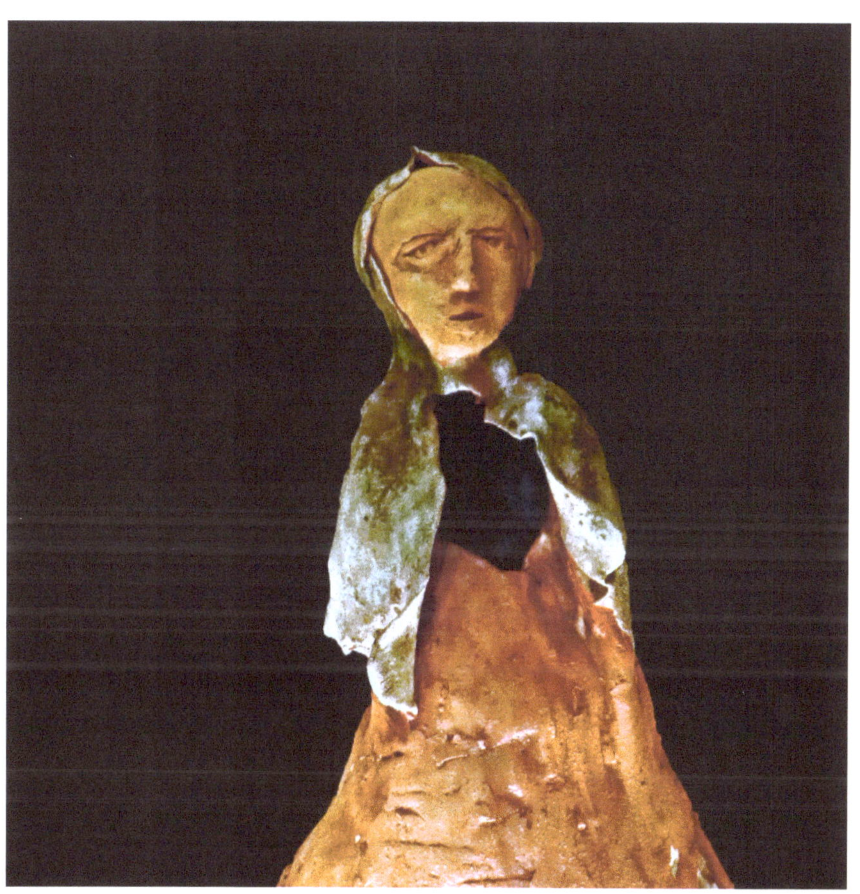

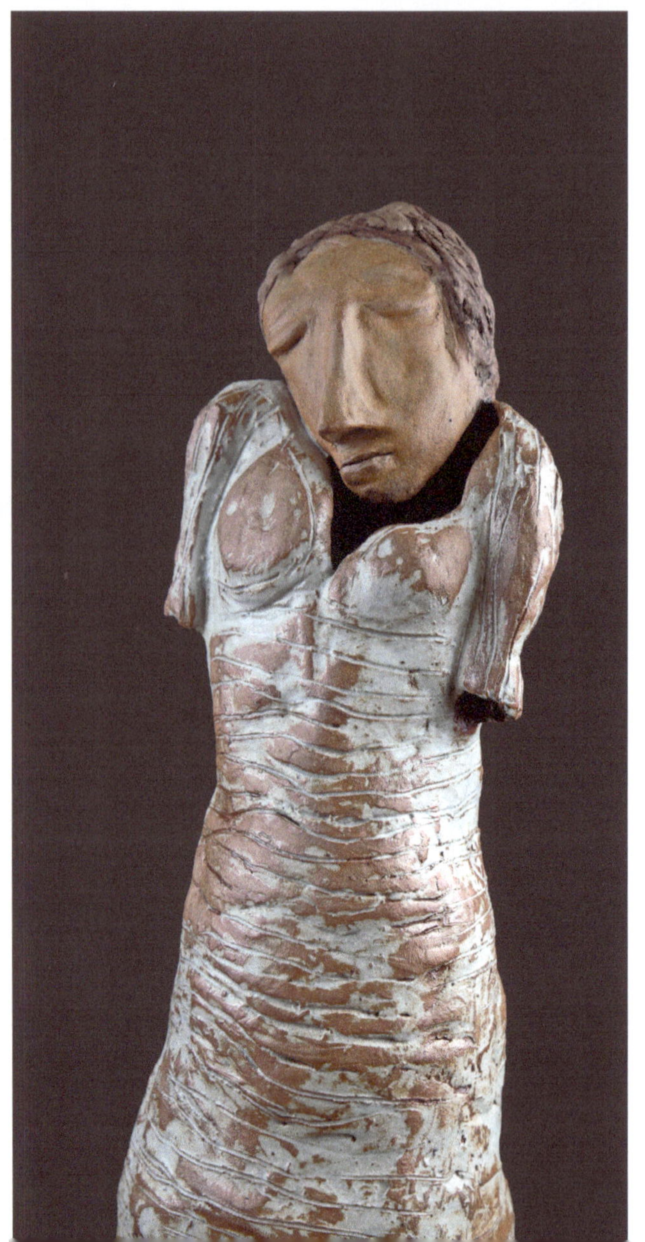

Now that the wind
has turned nameless
every person I pass
holds a secret hymn
love song.

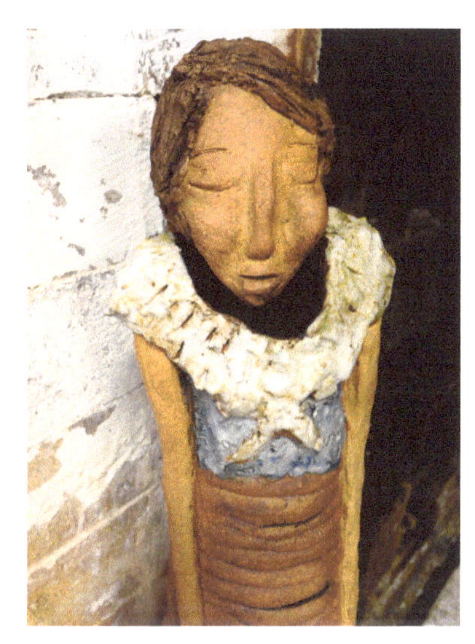

Amid the bramble
parched wind
summer's inferno of kisses
I cleave to your soil
am servant twice over
for the tulips you nest in me.

Too old to be young
too young to be old
I set time on a new axis
warn it not to beg.
Become the pole star
tethered to a strange galaxy.

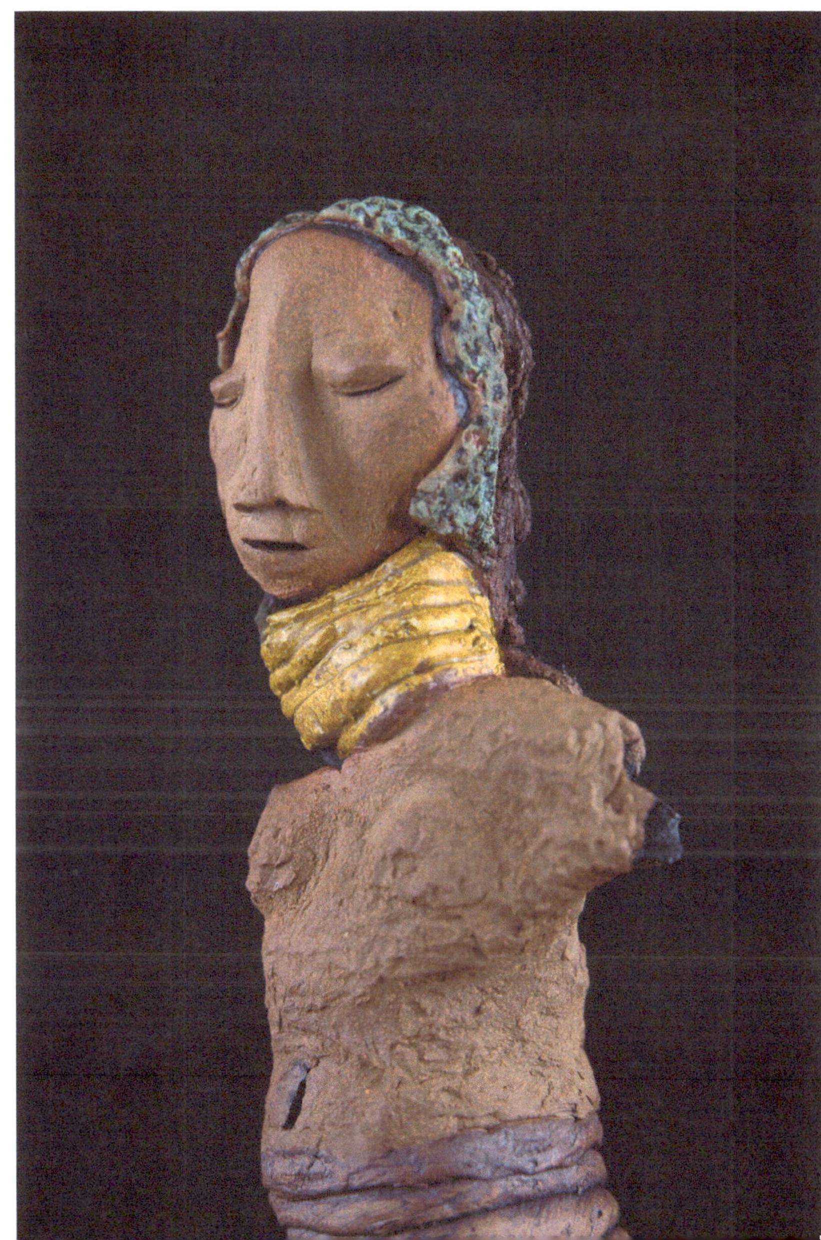

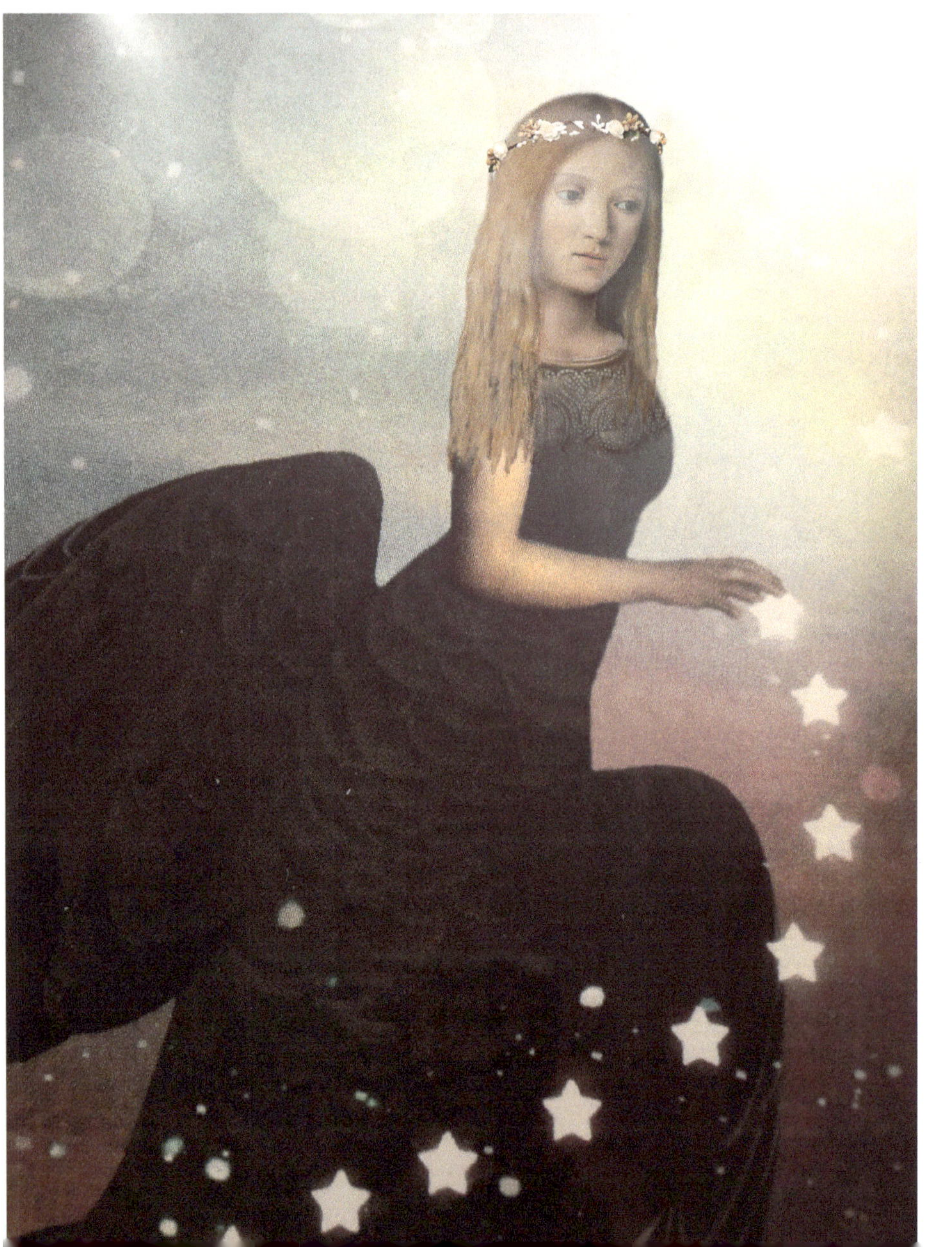

When I walk the path of stones
is any destination final?
Things come, things go.
But the moon, the stars
the hillside burnished with autumn
the snow that melts in my mouth
white as cake.

You unravel me
you unravel me
stab my body
with the penance of fuchsia.

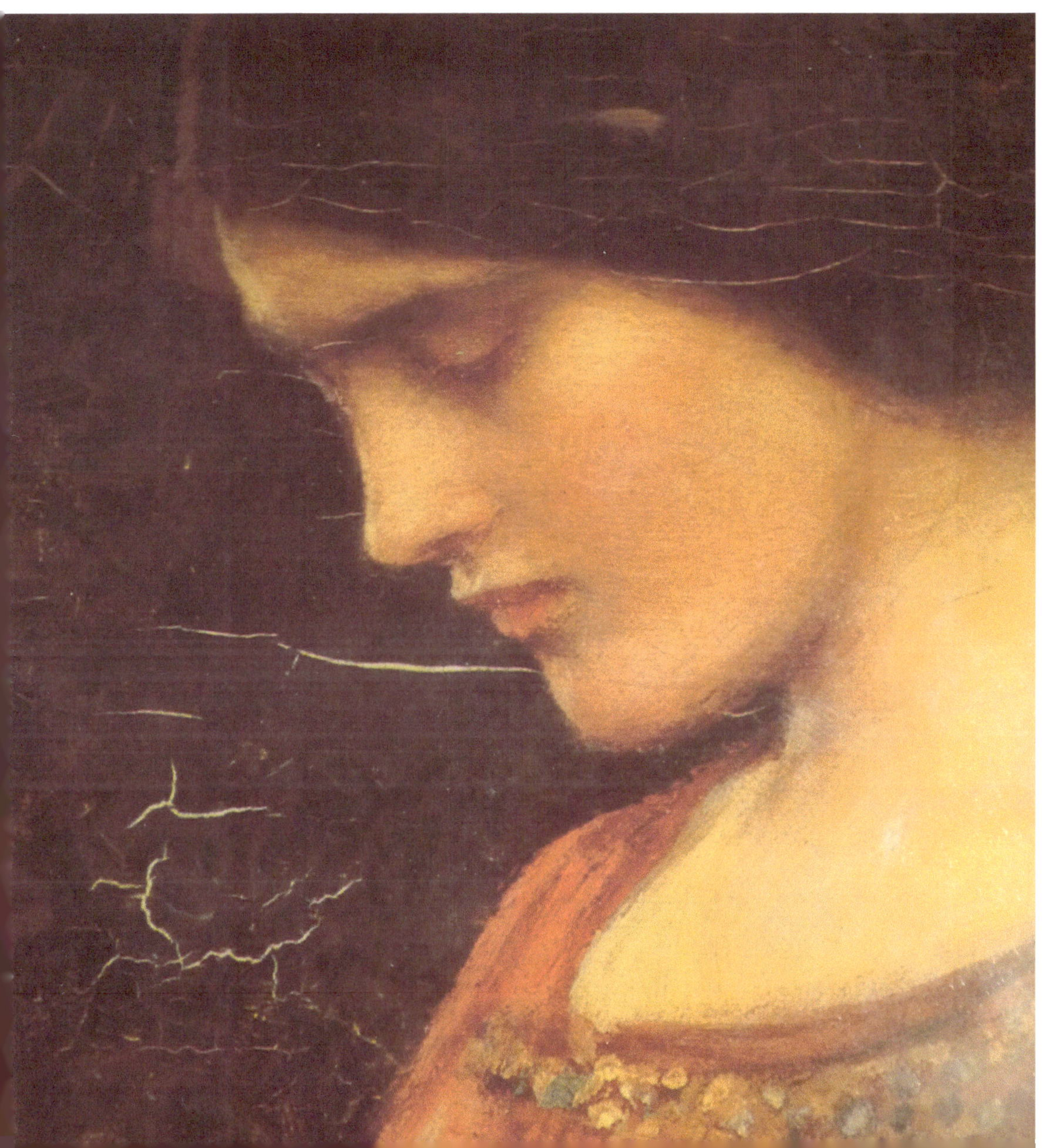

Toni Thomas's poems have been published in Austria, Spain, New Zealand, Ireland, Canada, England, Scotland, and Australia. In the United States her work has appeared in over fifty literary magazines including Prairie Schooner, North Dakota Quartely, Hayden's Ferry Review, the Minnesota Review, Notre Dame Review, Poetry East, and more. The recipient of several poetry awards, her work has twice been nominated for a Pushcart prize. She has published nine collections of poems and two children's books.

Her figurative clay sculptures have been shown in gallery and museum exhibits in Oregon and Chicago, displayed in literary magazines, and housed in private collections in the U.S. and England. Her short documentary *One of Us* was shown at the Trans-ideology: Nostalgia festival in Berlin and at the Museum of Contemporary Art in Taipei.